50 New Orleans Creole Cooking Recipes for Home

By: Kelly Johnson

Table of Contents

- Gumbo
- Jambalaya
- Shrimp Creole
- Red Beans and Rice
- Crawfish Étouffée
- Chicken and Sausage Gumbo
- Dirty Rice
- Seafood Gumbo
- Creole Shrimp Pasta
- Chicken Creole
- Oyster Po' Boy
- Muffuletta Sandwich
- Shrimp and Grits
- Cajun Shrimp Alfredo
- Blackened Catfish
- Crab Cakes
- Cajun Chicken Pasta
- Cajun Fried Chicken
- Creole Meatloaf
- Creole Chicken Salad
- Shrimp Po' Boy
- Cajun Shrimp and Corn Soup
- Crawfish Boil
- Cajun Crab Dip
- Cajun Cornbread
- Cajun Dirty Shrimp
- Cajun Shrimp Scampi
- Cajun Crawfish Pie
- Cajun Roasted Potatoes
- Cajun Blackened Salmon
- Cajun Stuffed Peppers
- Cajun Seafood Pasta
- Cajun Gumbo Soup
- Creole Shrimp and Sausage Jambalaya
- Blackened Redfish

- Cajun Chicken and Sausage Pasta
- Cajun Shrimp Tacos
- Cajun Stuffed Chicken Breast
- Cajun Baked Catfish
- Cajun Grilled Shrimp Skewers
- Cajun Chicken and Rice
- Cajun Shrimp and Sausage Gumbo
- Cajun Crab Salad
- Cajun Shrimp and Sausage Skillet
- Creole Stuffed Bell Peppers
- Cajun Sausage and Shrimp Alfredo
- Cajun Shrimp and Sausage Pasta Bake
- Cajun Fried Oysters
- Cajun Blackened Chicken
- Creole-style BBQ Shrimp

Gumbo

Ingredients:

- 1/2 cup vegetable oil
- 1/2 cup all-purpose flour
- 1 large onion, chopped
- 1 bell pepper, chopped
- 2 celery stalks, chopped
- 4 cloves garlic, minced
- 1 pound andouille sausage, sliced
- 1 pound chicken thighs, cut into bite-sized pieces
- 1 pound shrimp, peeled and deveined
- 1 can (14.5 ounces) diced tomatoes
- 4 cups chicken broth
- 1 teaspoon dried thyme
- 1 teaspoon dried oregano
- 1 teaspoon paprika
- 1/2 teaspoon cayenne pepper (adjust to taste)
- Salt and pepper to taste
- Cooked white rice, for serving
- Chopped green onions, for garnish
- File powder (optional), for serving

Instructions:

Make the Roux:
- In a large Dutch oven or heavy-bottomed pot, heat vegetable oil over medium heat.
- Gradually whisk in flour, stirring constantly to combine.
- Continue cooking, stirring frequently, until the roux reaches a dark brown color, similar to milk chocolate, about 30-40 minutes. Be careful not to burn it.

Sauté Vegetables:
- Add chopped onion, bell pepper, celery, and minced garlic to the roux. Cook, stirring frequently, until vegetables are softened, about 5-7 minutes.

Add Sausage and Chicken:
- Stir in sliced andouille sausage and chicken pieces. Cook until chicken is browned on all sides, about 5 minutes.

Add Tomatoes and Seasonings:

- Pour in diced tomatoes (with their juices) and chicken broth.
- Stir in dried thyme, dried oregano, paprika, cayenne pepper, salt, and pepper.

Simmer:
- Bring the mixture to a simmer, then reduce heat to low. Cover and let it simmer for about 30 minutes to allow the flavors to meld together.

Add Shrimp:
- Once the chicken is cooked through and tender, add peeled and deveined shrimp to the pot. Cook for an additional 5-7 minutes, or until shrimp turn pink and opaque.

Adjust Seasonings:
- Taste the gumbo and adjust seasoning if necessary. Add more salt, pepper, or cayenne pepper to taste.

Serve:
- Serve the gumbo hot over cooked white rice.
- Garnish with chopped green onions and sprinkle with file powder (if using) for added flavor.
- Enjoy this delicious and hearty New Orleans Gumbo!

This traditional New Orleans Gumbo is rich, flavorful, and perfect for sharing with family and friends. Adjust the spice level to your preference and savor the taste of Louisiana cuisine!

Jambalaya

Ingredients:

- 1 pound boneless, skinless chicken thighs, cut into bite-sized pieces
- 1 pound andouille sausage, sliced
- 1 large onion, diced
- 1 bell pepper, diced
- 2 celery stalks, diced
- 3 cloves garlic, minced
- 1 can (14.5 ounces) diced tomatoes
- 2 cups long-grain white rice
- 4 cups chicken broth
- 2 teaspoons Cajun seasoning
- 1 teaspoon dried thyme
- 1 teaspoon dried oregano
- 1 teaspoon paprika
- 1/2 teaspoon cayenne pepper (adjust to taste)
- Salt and black pepper to taste
- Chopped green onions, for garnish
- Chopped fresh parsley, for garnish

Instructions:

Sauté Chicken and Sausage:
- In a large Dutch oven or heavy-bottomed pot, heat some oil over medium-high heat.
- Add the chicken thighs and andouille sausage slices. Cook until the chicken is browned on all sides and sausage is slightly caramelized, about 5-7 minutes. Remove from the pot and set aside.

Sauté Vegetables:
- In the same pot, add a bit more oil if needed. Add the diced onion, bell pepper, celery, and minced garlic. Sauté until the vegetables are softened, about 5 minutes.

Add Tomatoes and Spices:
- Stir in the diced tomatoes (with their juices), Cajun seasoning, dried thyme, dried oregano, paprika, and cayenne pepper. Cook for another 2 minutes, stirring frequently.

Add Rice and Broth:

- Add the long-grain white rice to the pot, stirring to coat it with the vegetable and spice mixture.
- Pour in the chicken broth and return the cooked chicken and sausage to the pot. Stir everything together.

Simmer:
- Bring the mixture to a boil, then reduce the heat to low. Cover the pot and let it simmer for about 20-25 minutes, or until the rice is cooked and has absorbed the liquid.

Adjust Seasonings:
- Taste the jambalaya and adjust the seasoning with salt, black pepper, and additional Cajun seasoning if needed.

Serve:
- Once the rice is cooked and the flavors have melded together, remove the pot from the heat.
- Serve the jambalaya hot, garnished with chopped green onions and fresh parsley.

Enjoy this classic Jambalaya recipe, packed with savory flavors and perfect for a taste of New Orleans at home!

Shrimp Creole

Ingredients:

- 1 pound large shrimp, peeled and deveined
- 1 tablespoon olive oil
- 1 onion, diced
- 1 bell pepper, diced
- 2 celery stalks, diced
- 3 cloves garlic, minced
- 1 can (14.5 ounces) diced tomatoes
- 1 can (8 ounces) tomato sauce
- 1 cup chicken broth
- 2 teaspoons Creole seasoning
- 1 teaspoon paprika
- 1/2 teaspoon dried thyme
- 1/2 teaspoon dried oregano
- 1/4 teaspoon cayenne pepper (adjust to taste)
- Salt and black pepper to taste
- Cooked white rice, for serving
- Chopped fresh parsley, for garnish

Instructions:

Sauté Vegetables:
- In a large skillet or Dutch oven, heat olive oil over medium heat. Add diced onion, bell pepper, and celery. Cook until vegetables are softened, about 5-7 minutes.

Add Garlic and Spices:
- Add minced garlic to the skillet and cook for another minute until fragrant. Stir in Creole seasoning, paprika, dried thyme, dried oregano, and cayenne pepper. Cook for another minute to toast the spices.

Add Tomatoes and Sauce:
- Pour in diced tomatoes (with their juices), tomato sauce, and chicken broth. Stir to combine.

Simmer:
- Bring the mixture to a simmer, then reduce heat to low. Let it simmer uncovered for about 15-20 minutes to allow the flavors to meld together and the sauce to thicken slightly.

Cook Shrimp:

- Once the sauce has thickened, add the peeled and deveined shrimp to the skillet. Cook until the shrimp are pink and opaque, about 3-5 minutes. Be careful not to overcook them.

Adjust Seasonings:
- Taste the Shrimp Creole and adjust the seasoning with salt, black pepper, and additional Creole seasoning if needed.

Serve:
- Serve the Shrimp Creole hot over cooked white rice.
- Garnish with chopped fresh parsley for a pop of color and added flavor.

Enjoy this flavorful and spicy Shrimp Creole, perfect for a taste of New Orleans cuisine in the comfort of your own home!

Red Beans and Rice

Ingredients:

- 1 pound dried red kidney beans
- 1 large onion, chopped
- 1 bell pepper, chopped
- 2 celery stalks, chopped
- 4 cloves garlic, minced
- 1 pound Andouille sausage, sliced
- 4 cups chicken broth
- 2 bay leaves
- 1 teaspoon dried thyme
- 1 teaspoon dried oregano
- 1/2 teaspoon cayenne pepper (adjust to taste)
- Salt and black pepper to taste
- Cooked white rice, for serving
- Chopped green onions, for garnish

Instructions:

Soak the Beans:
- Rinse the dried red kidney beans under cold water and remove any debris. Place them in a large bowl and cover with water. Let them soak overnight, or use the quick soak method by boiling them for 2 minutes, then removing from heat and letting them soak for 1 hour.

Sauté Vegetables:
- In a large Dutch oven or heavy-bottomed pot, heat some oil over medium heat. Add the chopped onion, bell pepper, celery, and minced garlic. Sauté until the vegetables are softened, about 5-7 minutes.

Add Sausage and Spices:
- Add the sliced Andouille sausage to the pot and cook until browned, about 5 minutes.
- Stir in the bay leaves, dried thyme, dried oregano, cayenne pepper, salt, and black pepper. Cook for another minute, stirring frequently.

Cook Beans:
- Drain the soaked beans and add them to the pot.
- Pour in the chicken broth, ensuring that the beans are fully submerged.

- Bring the mixture to a boil, then reduce the heat to low. Cover the pot and let it simmer for about 1.5 to 2 hours, or until the beans are tender and creamy, stirring occasionally.

Mash Beans (Optional):
- If desired, use a potato masher to lightly mash some of the beans against the side of the pot. This will help thicken the mixture and give it a creamier texture.

Adjust Seasonings:
- Taste the Red Beans and Rice and adjust the seasoning with salt, black pepper, and additional cayenne pepper if desired.

Serve:
- Serve the Red Beans and Rice hot over cooked white rice.
- Garnish with chopped green onions before serving.

Enjoy this hearty and flavorful Red Beans and Rice, a staple of New Orleans cuisine, served as a main dish or side dish alongside your favorite Cajun or Creole dishes!

Crawfish Étouffée

Ingredients:

- 1/2 cup unsalted butter
- 1/2 cup all-purpose flour
- 1 large onion, diced
- 1 bell pepper, diced
- 2 celery stalks, diced
- 4 cloves garlic, minced
- 1 pound cooked crawfish tails, with fat
- 2 cups seafood or chicken broth
- 1 can (14.5 ounces) diced tomatoes
- 2 bay leaves
- 1 teaspoon dried thyme
- 1 teaspoon paprika
- 1/2 teaspoon cayenne pepper (adjust to taste)
- Salt and black pepper to taste
- Cooked white rice, for serving
- Chopped green onions, for garnish
- Chopped fresh parsley, for garnish

Instructions:

Prepare Roux:
- In a large Dutch oven or heavy-bottomed pot, melt the unsalted butter over medium heat. Gradually whisk in the all-purpose flour to create a roux. Cook the roux, stirring constantly, until it turns a golden brown color, about 10-15 minutes. Be careful not to burn it.

Sauté Vegetables:
- Add the diced onion, bell pepper, celery, and minced garlic to the roux. Sauté until the vegetables are softened, about 5-7 minutes.

Add Crawfish and Broth:
- Stir in the cooked crawfish tails (with fat) and seafood or chicken broth. Bring the mixture to a simmer.

Season:
- Add the diced tomatoes (with their juices), bay leaves, dried thyme, paprika, cayenne pepper, salt, and black pepper to the pot. Stir to combine.

Simmer:

- Reduce the heat to low and let the Crawfish Étouffée simmer, uncovered, for about 20-30 minutes, stirring occasionally. This allows the flavors to meld together and the sauce to thicken.

Adjust Seasonings:
- Taste the Crawfish Étouffée and adjust the seasoning with salt, black pepper, and additional cayenne pepper if desired.

Serve:
- Serve the Crawfish Étouffée hot over cooked white rice.
- Garnish with chopped green onions and chopped fresh parsley before serving.

Enjoy this flavorful and comforting Crawfish Étouffée, a classic Cajun dish that's perfect for sharing with family and friends!

Chicken and Sausage Gumbo

Ingredients:

- 1/2 cup vegetable oil
- 1/2 cup all-purpose flour
- 1 large onion, diced
- 1 bell pepper, diced
- 2 celery stalks, diced
- 4 cloves garlic, minced
- 1 pound andouille sausage, sliced
- 1 pound boneless, skinless chicken thighs, cut into bite-sized pieces
- 6 cups chicken broth
- 1 can (14.5 ounces) diced tomatoes
- 2 bay leaves
- 1 teaspoon dried thyme
- 1 teaspoon dried oregano
- 1 teaspoon paprika
- 1/2 teaspoon cayenne pepper (adjust to taste)
- Salt and black pepper to taste
- Cooked white rice, for serving
- Chopped green onions, for garnish

Instructions:

Prepare Roux:
- In a large Dutch oven or heavy-bottomed pot, heat vegetable oil over medium heat. Gradually whisk in all-purpose flour to create a roux. Cook the roux, stirring constantly, until it turns a dark brown color, similar to milk chocolate, about 20-30 minutes. Be careful not to burn it.

Sauté Vegetables:
- Add the diced onion, bell pepper, celery, and minced garlic to the roux. Sauté until the vegetables are softened, about 5-7 minutes.

Add Sausage and Chicken:
- Stir in the sliced andouille sausage and chicken pieces. Cook until the chicken is browned on all sides, about 5 minutes.

Add Broth and Seasonings:
- Pour in the chicken broth, ensuring that the meat and vegetables are fully submerged.

- Add the diced tomatoes (with their juices), bay leaves, dried thyme, dried oregano, paprika, cayenne pepper, salt, and black pepper to the pot. Stir to combine.

Simmer:
- Bring the mixture to a simmer, then reduce the heat to low. Cover the pot and let the Chicken and Sausage Gumbo simmer for about 1 hour, stirring occasionally. This allows the flavors to meld together.

Adjust Seasonings:
- Taste the gumbo and adjust the seasoning with salt, black pepper, and additional cayenne pepper if desired.

Serve:
- Serve the Chicken and Sausage Gumbo hot over cooked white rice.
- Garnish with chopped green onions before serving.

Enjoy this flavorful and hearty Chicken and Sausage Gumbo, a classic Cajun dish that's perfect for sharing with family and friends!

Dirty Rice

Ingredients:

- 1 pound ground pork or ground beef
- 1 tablespoon vegetable oil
- 1 large onion, diced
- 1 bell pepper, diced
- 2 celery stalks, diced
- 4 cloves garlic, minced
- 1 cup long-grain white rice
- 2 cups chicken broth
- 2 bay leaves
- 1 teaspoon dried thyme
- 1 teaspoon paprika
- 1/2 teaspoon cayenne pepper (adjust to taste)
- Salt and black pepper to taste
- Chopped green onions, for garnish

Instructions:

Cook Meat:
- In a large skillet or Dutch oven, heat vegetable oil over medium heat. Add ground pork or ground beef and cook until browned and cooked through, breaking it up with a spoon as it cooks. Remove excess fat if needed.

Sauté Vegetables:
- Add the diced onion, bell pepper, celery, and minced garlic to the skillet with the cooked meat. Sauté until the vegetables are softened, about 5-7 minutes.

Add Rice and Seasonings:
- Stir in the long-grain white rice, bay leaves, dried thyme, paprika, cayenne pepper, salt, and black pepper. Cook for another 2 minutes, stirring frequently.

Add Broth:
- Pour in the chicken broth, ensuring that the rice and meat mixture is fully submerged.

Simmer:
- Bring the mixture to a boil, then reduce the heat to low. Cover the skillet or Dutch oven and let the Dirty Rice simmer for about 20-25 minutes, or until the rice is cooked and has absorbed the liquid.

Adjust Seasonings:
- Taste the Dirty Rice and adjust the seasoning with salt, black pepper, and additional cayenne pepper if desired.

Serve:
- Serve the Dirty Rice hot, garnished with chopped green onions.

Enjoy this flavorful and comforting Dirty Rice, a classic Cajun dish that's perfect as a side or main dish!

Seafood Gumbo

Ingredients:

- 1/2 cup vegetable oil
- 1/2 cup all-purpose flour
- 1 large onion, diced
- 1 bell pepper, diced
- 2 celery stalks, diced
- 4 cloves garlic, minced
- 1 pound shrimp, peeled and deveined
- 1 pound crabmeat
- 1 pound okra, sliced (fresh or frozen)
- 1 can (14.5 ounces) diced tomatoes
- 8 cups seafood or chicken broth
- 2 bay leaves
- 1 teaspoon dried thyme
- 1 teaspoon dried oregano
- 1 teaspoon paprika
- 1/2 teaspoon cayenne pepper (adjust to taste)
- Salt and black pepper to taste
- Cooked white rice, for serving
- Chopped green onions, for garnish

Instructions:

Prepare Roux:
- In a large Dutch oven or heavy-bottomed pot, heat vegetable oil over medium heat. Gradually whisk in all-purpose flour to create a roux. Cook the roux, stirring constantly, until it turns a dark brown color, similar to milk chocolate, about 20-30 minutes. Be careful not to burn it.

Sauté Vegetables:
- Add the diced onion, bell pepper, celery, and minced garlic to the roux. Sauté until the vegetables are softened, about 5-7 minutes.

Add Seafood and Okra:
- Stir in the peeled and deveined shrimp, crabmeat, and sliced okra. Cook for about 5 minutes, until the shrimp are pink and cooked through.

Add Tomatoes and Broth:
- Pour in the diced tomatoes (with their juices) and seafood or chicken broth. Stir to combine.

Seasonings:
- Add the bay leaves, dried thyme, dried oregano, paprika, cayenne pepper, salt, and black pepper to the pot. Stir to combine.

Simmer:
- Bring the Seafood Gumbo to a simmer, then reduce the heat to low. Cover the pot and let it simmer for about 30-40 minutes, stirring occasionally. This allows the flavors to meld together and the gumbo to thicken.

Adjust Seasonings:
- Taste the Seafood Gumbo and adjust the seasoning with salt, black pepper, and additional cayenne pepper if desired.

Serve:
- Serve the Seafood Gumbo hot over cooked white rice.
- Garnish with chopped green onions before serving.

Enjoy this flavorful and comforting Seafood Gumbo, packed with shrimp, crabmeat, and okra, perfect for a taste of Louisiana cuisine!

Creole Shrimp Pasta

Ingredients:

- 1 pound shrimp, peeled and deveined
- 8 ounces pasta (such as linguine or fettuccine)
- 2 tablespoons olive oil
- 1 onion, finely chopped
- 1 bell pepper, diced
- 2 celery stalks, diced
- 3 cloves garlic, minced
- 1 can (14.5 ounces) diced tomatoes
- 1 teaspoon paprika
- 1/2 teaspoon dried thyme
- 1/2 teaspoon dried oregano
- 1/4 teaspoon cayenne pepper (adjust to taste)
- Salt and pepper to taste
- Fresh parsley, chopped (for garnish)
- Lemon wedges (for serving)

Instructions:

Cook the pasta according to package instructions until al dente. Drain and set aside.

In a large skillet, heat the olive oil over medium heat. Add the onion, bell pepper, and celery. Cook until softened, about 5 minutes.

Add the minced garlic to the skillet and cook for an additional minute until fragrant.

Stir in the diced tomatoes (with their juices), paprika, thyme, oregano, and cayenne pepper. Season with salt and pepper to taste. Let the mixture simmer for about 10 minutes, allowing the flavors to meld together.

Add the shrimp to the skillet and cook until they turn pink and opaque, about 3-4 minutes.

Once the shrimp are cooked through, add the cooked pasta to the skillet. Toss everything together until the pasta is coated evenly with the sauce.

Serve the Creole shrimp pasta hot, garnished with chopped parsley and lemon wedges on the side for squeezing over the dish.

Enjoy your flavorful Creole shrimp pasta!

Chicken Creole

Ingredients:

- 4 boneless, skinless chicken breasts, cut into chunks
- Salt and pepper to taste
- 2 tablespoons olive oil
- 1 onion, finely chopped
- 1 bell pepper, diced
- 2 celery stalks, diced
- 3 cloves garlic, minced
- 1 can (14.5 ounces) diced tomatoes
- 1 can (8 ounces) tomato sauce
- 1 cup chicken broth
- 2 teaspoons Creole seasoning (store-bought or homemade)
- 1/2 teaspoon dried thyme
- 1/2 teaspoon dried oregano
- 1/4 teaspoon cayenne pepper (adjust to taste)
- 1 bay leaf
- 2 tablespoons all-purpose flour
- 2 tablespoons water
- Cooked rice, for serving
- Fresh parsley, chopped (for garnish)

Instructions:

Season the chicken chunks with salt and pepper to taste.
In a large skillet or Dutch oven, heat the olive oil over medium heat. Add the chicken pieces and cook until browned on all sides, about 5 minutes. Remove the chicken from the skillet and set aside.
In the same skillet, add the chopped onion, bell pepper, and celery. Cook until softened, about 5 minutes.
Add the minced garlic to the skillet and cook for an additional minute until fragrant.
Stir in the diced tomatoes (with their juices), tomato sauce, chicken broth, Creole seasoning, thyme, oregano, cayenne pepper, and bay leaf. Bring the mixture to a simmer.

Return the cooked chicken to the skillet, nestling it into the sauce. Cover and let it simmer gently for about 20-25 minutes, or until the chicken is cooked through and tender.

In a small bowl, mix together the flour and water to create a slurry. Stir the slurry into the chicken mixture to thicken the sauce. Let it simmer for an additional 5 minutes.

Serve the Chicken Creole hot over cooked rice, garnished with chopped parsley.

Enjoy your flavorful and comforting Chicken Creole!

Oyster Po' Boy

Ingredients:

For the remoulade sauce:

- 1/2 cup mayonnaise
- 2 tablespoons Creole mustard (or Dijon mustard)
- 1 tablespoon prepared horseradish
- 1 tablespoon ketchup
- 1 tablespoon hot sauce (such as Tabasco)
- 2 cloves garlic, minced
- 1 tablespoon chopped fresh parsley
- 1 tablespoon chopped green onions
- 1 teaspoon paprika
- Salt and pepper to taste

For the Po' Boy:

- 1 pound fresh oysters, shucked
- 1 cup all-purpose flour
- 1 teaspoon paprika
- 1/2 teaspoon garlic powder
- Salt and pepper to taste
- Vegetable oil, for frying
- French baguette or French bread, cut into sandwich-sized portions
- Lettuce leaves
- Sliced tomatoes
- Sliced pickles (optional)
- Lemon wedges (for serving)

Instructions:

Prepare the remoulade sauce by mixing together all the ingredients in a bowl until well combined. Adjust seasoning to taste. Cover and refrigerate until ready to use.

In a shallow dish, mix together the flour, paprika, garlic powder, salt, and pepper. Dredge the oysters in the seasoned flour mixture, shaking off any excess.

In a large skillet or deep fryer, heat vegetable oil to 350°F (180°C). Fry the oysters in batches until golden brown and crispy, about 2-3 minutes per batch. Remove with a slotted spoon and drain on paper towels.

Slice the baguette or French bread lengthwise, leaving one side attached to form a hinge. Spread a generous amount of remoulade sauce on both halves of the bread.

Arrange lettuce leaves on the bottom half of the bread. Top with sliced tomatoes, fried oysters, and pickles if using.

Close the sandwich with the top half of the bread and press down gently.

Serve the Oyster Po' Boy sandwiches immediately, accompanied by lemon wedges for squeezing over the oysters.

Enjoy your flavorful and crispy Oyster Po' Boy sandwiches!

Muffuletta Sandwich

Ingredients:

For the Olive Salad:

- 1 cup pitted green olives, chopped
- 1 cup pitted black olives, chopped
- 1/4 cup chopped pickled vegetables (like cauliflower, carrots, celery)
- 2 tablespoons capers, drained
- 2 cloves garlic, minced
- 1/4 cup chopped fresh parsley
- 2 tablespoons red wine vinegar
- 1/4 cup extra virgin olive oil
- Salt and pepper to taste

For the Sandwich:

- 1 round loaf of Italian bread (about 10 inches in diameter)
- 4 ounces thinly sliced Genoa salami
- 4 ounces thinly sliced mortadella
- 4 ounces thinly sliced ham
- 4 ounces thinly sliced provolone cheese

Instructions:

Prepare the olive salad by combining the chopped green olives, black olives, pickled vegetables, capers, garlic, parsley, red wine vinegar, and olive oil in a bowl. Season with salt and pepper to taste. Mix well and set aside for at least 30 minutes to allow the flavors to meld.

Cut the round loaf of Italian bread in half horizontally. Hollow out some of the bread from the top and bottom halves to create space for the filling.

Spread a generous layer of the olive salad on the bottom half of the bread.

Layer the Genoa salami, mortadella, ham, and provolone cheese on top of the olive salad.

Spread another layer of olive salad on top of the cheese.

Place the top half of the bread over the filling and press down gently to compact the sandwich.

Wrap the sandwich tightly in plastic wrap and refrigerate for at least 1 hour, or overnight, to allow the flavors to meld and the sandwich to firm up.

When ready to serve, unwrap the sandwich and cut it into quarters or wedges. Serve the Muffuletta sandwich cold or at room temperature, accompanied by your favorite side dishes or pickles.

Enjoy your homemade Muffuletta sandwich!

Shrimp and Grits

Ingredients:

For the Shrimp:

- 1 pound large shrimp, peeled and deveined
- 2 tablespoons Cajun seasoning (or to taste)
- 2 tablespoons olive oil
- 4 cloves garlic, minced
- 1 onion, finely chopped
- 1 bell pepper, diced
- 1 cup chicken broth
- 1 cup diced tomatoes (canned or fresh)
- Salt and pepper to taste
- Chopped green onions or parsley for garnish

For the Grits:

- 1 cup stone-ground grits
- 4 cups water
- 1 cup milk
- 4 tablespoons unsalted butter
- Salt to taste
- 1 cup shredded cheddar cheese (optional)

Instructions:

Start by preparing the grits. In a medium saucepan, bring the water and milk to a boil over medium-high heat.

Slowly whisk in the grits, reduce the heat to low, and cover the saucepan. Let the grits simmer, stirring occasionally, for about 20-25 minutes, or until thickened and creamy.

Stir in the butter and salt. If desired, add the shredded cheddar cheese and mix until melted and combined. Keep warm while you prepare the shrimp.

In a large skillet, heat the olive oil over medium heat. Add the minced garlic and sauté for about 1 minute, until fragrant.

Add the chopped onion and bell pepper to the skillet and cook until softened, about 5 minutes.

Season the shrimp with Cajun seasoning, salt, and pepper. Add the seasoned shrimp to the skillet and cook until they turn pink, about 2-3 minutes per side.

Pour in the chicken broth and diced tomatoes, and let the mixture simmer for an additional 5 minutes, allowing the flavors to meld and the sauce to thicken slightly.

Taste and adjust the seasoning if necessary.

To serve, spoon the creamy grits into bowls and top with the cooked shrimp and sauce.

Garnish with chopped green onions or parsley.

Serve immediately and enjoy your delicious Shrimp and Grits!

Feel free to customize this recipe by adding other ingredients such as bacon, sausage, or additional vegetables to the shrimp mixture.

Cajun Shrimp Alfredo

Ingredients:

For the Cajun Shrimp:

- 1 pound large shrimp, peeled and deveined
- 2 tablespoons Cajun seasoning
- 2 tablespoons olive oil
- 4 cloves garlic, minced
- Salt and pepper to taste

For the Alfredo Sauce:

- 1/2 cup unsalted butter
- 4 cloves garlic, minced
- 2 cups heavy cream
- 1 cup grated Parmesan cheese
- Salt and pepper to taste
- 1 teaspoon dried Italian seasoning (optional)
- 1/4 teaspoon red pepper flakes (optional)

For the Pasta:

- 12 ounces fettuccine or pasta of your choice
- Chopped fresh parsley for garnish
- Grated Parmesan cheese for garnish

Instructions:

Cook the pasta according to the package instructions until al dente. Drain and set aside.
In a large skillet, heat the olive oil over medium-high heat. Add the minced garlic and sauté for about 1 minute until fragrant.
Add the shrimp to the skillet and sprinkle with Cajun seasoning, salt, and pepper. Cook the shrimp until they turn pink and opaque, about 2-3 minutes per side. Remove the shrimp from the skillet and set aside.

In the same skillet, melt the butter over medium heat. Add the minced garlic and cook for about 1 minute until fragrant.

Pour in the heavy cream and bring to a simmer. Cook for about 5 minutes, stirring occasionally, until the sauce begins to thicken slightly.

Stir in the grated Parmesan cheese until melted and well combined. Season the sauce with salt, pepper, dried Italian seasoning, and red pepper flakes, if using.

Add the cooked pasta to the skillet with the Alfredo sauce and toss until the pasta is well coated.

Gently stir in the cooked Cajun shrimp until evenly distributed throughout the pasta.

Cook for an additional 2-3 minutes, until the shrimp is heated through.

Remove from heat and garnish with chopped fresh parsley and grated Parmesan cheese.

Serve hot and enjoy your delicious Cajun Shrimp Alfredo!

Feel free to adjust the level of Cajun seasoning and red pepper flakes to suit your taste preferences. You can also add extra vegetables such as bell peppers, onions, or spinach to the dish for added flavor and nutrition.

Blackened Catfish

Ingredients:

- 4 catfish fillets (about 6-8 ounces each), skin removed
- 2 tablespoons paprika
- 1 tablespoon dried thyme
- 1 tablespoon dried oregano
- 1 tablespoon garlic powder
- 1 tablespoon onion powder
- 1 teaspoon cayenne pepper (adjust to taste)
- 1 teaspoon black pepper
- 1 teaspoon white pepper
- 1 teaspoon salt
- 4 tablespoons unsalted butter, melted
- Lemon wedges, for serving
- Chopped fresh parsley, for garnish (optional)

Instructions:

In a small bowl, mix together the paprika, dried thyme, dried oregano, garlic powder, onion powder, cayenne pepper, black pepper, white pepper, and salt to make the blackening seasoning.

Pat the catfish fillets dry with paper towels. Generously coat both sides of each fillet with the blackening seasoning mixture, pressing gently to adhere.

Heat a large cast-iron skillet or heavy-bottomed pan over medium-high heat until very hot.

Carefully add the melted butter to the hot skillet. Place the seasoned catfish fillets in the skillet, being careful not to overcrowd the pan. You may need to cook the fillets in batches, depending on the size of your skillet.

Cook the catfish fillets for about 3-4 minutes on each side, or until blackened and cooked through. The fish should easily flake with a fork when done.

Once cooked, transfer the blackened catfish fillets to a serving platter or individual plates.

Garnish with chopped fresh parsley, if desired, and serve hot with lemon wedges on the side.

Enjoy your delicious blackened catfish with your favorite side dishes such as rice, coleslaw, or vegetables.

This recipe delivers a spicy and flavorful dish, but feel free to adjust the amount of cayenne pepper according to your taste preferences.

Crab Cakes

Ingredients:

- 1 pound lump crab meat, picked over for shells
- 1/2 cup breadcrumbs (preferably fresh)
- 1/4 cup mayonnaise
- 1 large egg, lightly beaten
- 2 tablespoons chopped fresh parsley
- 2 green onions, finely chopped
- 1 tablespoon Dijon mustard
- 1 tablespoon Worcestershire sauce
- 1 teaspoon Old Bay seasoning (or more to taste)
- 1/2 teaspoon garlic powder
- Salt and pepper to taste
- 2 tablespoons unsalted butter, for frying
- Lemon wedges and tartar sauce, for serving

Instructions:

In a large mixing bowl, combine the lump crab meat, breadcrumbs, mayonnaise, beaten egg, chopped parsley, chopped green onions, Dijon mustard, Worcestershire sauce, Old Bay seasoning, garlic powder, salt, and pepper. Gently fold the mixture together until well combined, being careful not to break up the crab meat too much.
Once the mixture is well combined, shape it into crab cakes. Depending on your preference, you can make smaller cakes for appetizers or larger ones for main courses. Place the formed crab cakes on a baking sheet lined with parchment paper and refrigerate for at least 30 minutes to firm up.
Heat the butter in a large skillet over medium heat until melted and hot. Carefully place the crab cakes in the skillet, being careful not to overcrowd the pan. Cook the crab cakes for about 4-5 minutes on each side, or until golden brown and crispy.
Once the crab cakes are cooked through and nicely browned on both sides, transfer them to a plate lined with paper towels to drain any excess oil.
Serve the crab cakes hot with lemon wedges and tartar sauce on the side for dipping.
Enjoy your delicious homemade crab cakes as an appetizer, main course, or part of a seafood feast!

Feel free to adjust the seasonings and ingredients according to your taste preferences. You can also bake the crab cakes in a preheated oven at 375°F (190°C) for about 15-20 minutes instead of frying them if you prefer a healthier option.

Cajun Chicken Pasta

Ingredients:

- 8 ounces fettuccine or pasta of your choice
- 2 boneless, skinless chicken breasts, thinly sliced
- 2 tablespoons Cajun seasoning
- Salt and pepper to taste
- 2 tablespoons olive oil
- 1 red bell pepper, thinly sliced
- 1 green bell pepper, thinly sliced
- 1 small onion, thinly sliced
- 4 ounces mushrooms, sliced
- 3 cloves garlic, minced
- 1 cup heavy cream
- 1/2 cup grated Parmesan cheese
- Chopped fresh parsley for garnish (optional)

Instructions:

Cook the pasta according to the package instructions until al dente. Drain and set aside.

Season the thinly sliced chicken breasts with Cajun seasoning, salt, and pepper, making sure they're evenly coated.

Heat 1 tablespoon of olive oil in a large skillet over medium-high heat. Add the seasoned chicken slices to the skillet and cook for 5-6 minutes on each side, or until cooked through and no longer pink in the center. Remove the chicken from the skillet and set aside.

In the same skillet, add the remaining tablespoon of olive oil. Add the sliced bell peppers, onion, and mushrooms to the skillet. Cook, stirring occasionally, for about 5-6 minutes, or until the vegetables are tender.

Add the minced garlic to the skillet and cook for an additional 1 minute until fragrant.

Pour in the heavy cream and bring to a simmer. Cook for about 3-4 minutes, stirring occasionally, until the sauce thickens slightly.

Stir in the grated Parmesan cheese until melted and well combined.

Return the cooked chicken slices to the skillet with the creamy sauce and vegetables. Stir to coat the chicken evenly with the sauce.

Add the cooked pasta to the skillet and toss until well coated with the creamy Cajun sauce.

Cook for an additional 2-3 minutes, allowing the pasta to absorb the flavors of the sauce.

Garnish with chopped fresh parsley, if desired, and serve hot.

Enjoy your delicious Cajun Chicken Pasta!

Feel free to adjust the level of Cajun seasoning according to your taste preferences. You can also add more vegetables such as cherry tomatoes, spinach, or broccoli to the dish for added flavor and nutrition.

Cajun Fried Chicken

Ingredients:

For the Chicken:

- 2 lbs chicken pieces (such as drumsticks, thighs, or breasts), skin-on
- Salt and pepper to taste
- 2 cups buttermilk
- 2 tablespoons hot sauce (optional)
- Vegetable oil for frying

For the Cajun Seasoning:

- 2 tablespoons paprika
- 1 tablespoon garlic powder
- 1 tablespoon onion powder
- 1 tablespoon dried oregano
- 1 tablespoon dried thyme
- 1 tablespoon cayenne pepper (adjust to taste)
- 1 tablespoon black pepper
- 1 tablespoon white pepper
- 1 tablespoon salt

For the Coating:

- 1 1/2 cups all-purpose flour
- 1/2 cup cornstarch
- 1 tablespoon Cajun seasoning
- 1 teaspoon baking powder

Instructions:

In a large bowl, combine the buttermilk, hot sauce (if using), and a pinch of salt and pepper. Add the chicken pieces to the bowl, ensuring they are fully submerged in the buttermilk mixture. Cover the bowl with plastic wrap and refrigerate for at least 4 hours or overnight.
In a separate bowl, mix together all the ingredients for the Cajun seasoning.
In another bowl, whisk together the all-purpose flour, cornstarch, Cajun seasoning, and baking powder to create the coating mixture.

Remove the chicken pieces from the buttermilk marinade, allowing any excess liquid to drip off.
Coat each chicken piece thoroughly in the seasoned flour mixture, shaking off any excess.
Heat vegetable oil in a large skillet or Dutch oven to 350°F (175°C) for frying.
Carefully add the coated chicken pieces to the hot oil, making sure not to overcrowd the pan. Fry in batches if necessary.
Fry the chicken pieces for about 12-15 minutes, turning occasionally, until they are golden brown and crispy and the internal temperature reaches 165°F (75°C) for thighs and drumsticks or 170°F (77°C) for breasts.
Once cooked, remove the chicken from the oil and transfer to a wire rack or paper towel-lined plate to drain any excess oil.
Allow the chicken to rest for a few minutes before serving.
Serve the Cajun fried chicken hot with your favorite sides, such as mashed potatoes, coleslaw, or cornbread.
Enjoy your delicious homemade Cajun fried chicken!

Feel free to adjust the level of cayenne pepper in the Cajun seasoning to suit your taste preferences. You can also add additional spices or herbs for more flavor variation.

Creole Meatloaf

Ingredients:

- 1 1/2 pounds ground beef
- 1/2 pound ground pork (or sausage meat)
- 1 cup breadcrumbs
- 1 onion, finely chopped
- 1 green bell pepper, finely chopped
- 2 celery stalks, finely chopped
- 3 cloves garlic, minced
- 1/4 cup ketchup
- 2 tablespoons Creole or Cajun seasoning
- 1 tablespoon Worcestershire sauce
- 1 tablespoon Dijon mustard
- 2 eggs, beaten
- Salt and pepper to taste
- Cooking spray or olive oil, for greasing

For the Glaze:

- 1/4 cup ketchup
- 2 tablespoons brown sugar
- 1 tablespoon apple cider vinegar
- 1 teaspoon Creole or Cajun seasoning

Instructions:

Preheat the oven to 350°F (175°C). Grease a loaf pan with cooking spray or olive oil and set aside.

In a large mixing bowl, combine the ground beef, ground pork, breadcrumbs, chopped onion, chopped bell pepper, chopped celery, minced garlic, ketchup, Creole or Cajun seasoning, Worcestershire sauce, Dijon mustard, beaten eggs, salt, and pepper. Use your hands or a spoon to mix everything together until well combined.

Transfer the meat mixture into the greased loaf pan, pressing it down evenly.

In a small bowl, prepare the glaze by mixing together the ketchup, brown sugar, apple cider vinegar, and Creole or Cajun seasoning until smooth.

Spread the glaze evenly over the top of the meatloaf.

Place the loaf pan in the preheated oven and bake for about 1 hour to 1 hour 15 minutes, or until the meatloaf is cooked through and the top is nicely browned.
Once cooked, remove the meatloaf from the oven and let it rest for a few minutes before slicing.
Slice the meatloaf and serve hot, accompanied by your favorite sides such as mashed potatoes, green beans, or cornbread.
Enjoy your flavorful Creole meatloaf!

Feel free to customize this recipe by adding additional vegetables, such as carrots or mushrooms, or adjusting the level of spice according to your taste preferences.

Creole Chicken Salad

Ingredients:

For the Chicken:

- 2 boneless, skinless chicken breasts
- 1 tablespoon Cajun seasoning
- Salt and pepper to taste
- Olive oil for cooking

For the Salad:

- 4 cups mixed salad greens (such as lettuce, spinach, or arugula)
- 1 cup cherry tomatoes, halved
- 1 bell pepper, thinly sliced
- 1/2 red onion, thinly sliced
- 1/4 cup sliced black olives
- 1/4 cup chopped green onions
- 1/4 cup chopped fresh parsley

For the Dressing:

- 1/4 cup mayonnaise
- 2 tablespoons Creole mustard (or Dijon mustard)
- 1 tablespoon lemon juice
- 1 teaspoon Worcestershire sauce
- 1 teaspoon hot sauce (optional)
- Salt and pepper to taste

Instructions:

Preheat the oven to 375°F (190°C).
Season the chicken breasts with Cajun seasoning, salt, and pepper on both sides. Heat a drizzle of olive oil in a skillet over medium-high heat. Add the seasoned chicken breasts and cook for 3-4 minutes on each side until golden brown.

Transfer the skillet to the preheated oven and continue cooking the chicken breasts for another 15-20 minutes, or until they are cooked through and reach an internal temperature of 165°F (75°C). Once cooked, remove the chicken from the oven and let it rest for a few minutes before slicing.

While the chicken is cooking, prepare the salad ingredients. In a large salad bowl, combine the mixed salad greens, cherry tomatoes, bell pepper slices, red onion slices, black olives, green onions, and chopped parsley.

In a small bowl, whisk together the mayonnaise, Creole mustard, lemon juice, Worcestershire sauce, hot sauce (if using), salt, and pepper to make the dressing.

Slice the cooked chicken breasts into thin strips.

Add the sliced chicken to the salad bowl with the prepared vegetables.

Drizzle the dressing over the salad and toss gently to coat everything evenly.

Taste and adjust the seasoning if necessary.

Serve the Creole Chicken Salad immediately, garnished with extra chopped parsley or green onions if desired.

Enjoy your delicious and flavorful Creole-inspired chicken salad!

Feel free to customize this recipe by adding other ingredients such as avocado, cucumber, or boiled eggs to the salad. You can also adjust the level of spiciness by adding more or less Cajun seasoning and hot sauce to suit your taste preferences.

Shrimp Po' Boy

Ingredients:

For the Shrimp:

- 1 pound large shrimp, peeled and deveined
- 1 cup all-purpose flour
- 1 teaspoon Cajun seasoning
- 1/2 teaspoon garlic powder
- 1/2 teaspoon paprika
- Salt and pepper to taste
- Vegetable oil for frying

For the Remoulade Sauce:

- 1/2 cup mayonnaise
- 2 tablespoons Creole mustard (or Dijon mustard)
- 1 tablespoon ketchup
- 1 tablespoon prepared horseradish
- 1 tablespoon chopped fresh parsley
- 1 clove garlic, minced
- 1 teaspoon paprika
- 1 teaspoon hot sauce (adjust to taste)
- Salt and pepper to taste

For the Sandwich:

- French bread rolls (baguette), sliced horizontally
- Lettuce leaves
- Sliced tomatoes
- Sliced pickles
- Sliced red onion (optional)
- Lemon wedges for serving

Instructions:

Prepare the remoulade sauce by combining all the ingredients in a bowl. Mix well until smooth and creamy. Taste and adjust the seasoning if necessary. Cover the bowl and refrigerate the sauce until ready to use.

In a shallow dish, mix together the all-purpose flour, Cajun seasoning, garlic powder, paprika, salt, and pepper.

Heat vegetable oil in a deep skillet or Dutch oven over medium-high heat until it reaches 350°F (175°C).

While the oil is heating, coat the peeled and deveined shrimp in the seasoned flour mixture, shaking off any excess.

Carefully add the coated shrimp to the hot oil in batches, making sure not to overcrowd the pan. Fry the shrimp for about 2-3 minutes per side, or until they are golden brown and crispy. Remove the fried shrimp from the oil using a slotted spoon and transfer them to a plate lined with paper towels to drain any excess oil.

Once all the shrimp are fried, assemble the po' boy sandwiches. Spread a generous amount of remoulade sauce on the sliced French bread rolls.

Arrange the fried shrimp on the bottom half of each roll.

Top the shrimp with lettuce leaves, sliced tomatoes, pickles, and sliced red onion if desired.

Close the sandwiches with the top halves of the French bread rolls.

Serve the Shrimp Po' Boy sandwiches immediately, accompanied by lemon wedges for squeezing over the shrimp.

Enjoy your delicious homemade Shrimp Po' Boy sandwiches!

Feel free to customize your Shrimp Po' Boy with additional toppings such as coleslaw, avocado, or hot sauce according to your taste preferences.

Cajun Shrimp and Corn Soup

Ingredients:

- 1 pound shrimp, peeled and deveined
- 4 cups chicken or seafood broth
- 2 cups fresh or frozen corn kernels
- 1 onion, chopped
- 2 cloves garlic, minced
- 1 bell pepper, chopped
- 2 celery stalks, chopped
- 1 cup heavy cream
- 2 tablespoons Cajun seasoning
- 2 tablespoons all-purpose flour
- 2 tablespoons butter
- Salt and pepper to taste
- Chopped fresh parsley for garnish
- Cooked rice for serving (optional)

Instructions:

In a large pot, melt the butter over medium heat. Add the chopped onion, garlic, bell pepper, and celery. Sauté for 5-6 minutes, or until the vegetables are softened.
Sprinkle the flour over the vegetables and stir to combine. Cook for 1-2 minutes, stirring constantly, to create a roux.
Slowly pour in the chicken or seafood broth while stirring continuously to prevent lumps from forming.
Add the Cajun seasoning to the pot and stir well to incorporate.
Bring the soup to a simmer and let it cook for about 10-15 minutes, allowing the flavors to meld and the soup to thicken slightly.
Add the corn kernels to the pot and continue to simmer for another 5 minutes.
Stir in the heavy cream and let the soup simmer for an additional 5 minutes.
Add the peeled and deveined shrimp to the pot and cook for 3-4 minutes, or until the shrimp are pink and opaque.
Taste the soup and adjust the seasoning with salt and pepper if necessary.
Once the shrimp are cooked through, remove the pot from the heat.

Serve the Cajun Shrimp and Corn Soup hot, garnished with chopped fresh parsley. Optionally, serve over cooked rice for a heartier meal.
Enjoy your delicious and comforting Cajun Shrimp and Corn Soup!

Feel free to customize this recipe by adding other ingredients such as diced tomatoes, sliced okra, or smoked sausage for additional flavor and texture. You can also adjust the level of Cajun seasoning to suit your taste preferences.

Crawfish Boil

Ingredients:

- 30-40 pounds live crawfish (ideally, about 3-5 pounds per person)
- 10-15 quarts water
- 5 pounds small red potatoes
- 8 ears of corn, husked and halved
- 3 pounds smoked sausage, cut into chunks
- 2-3 onions, quartered
- 2-3 lemons, halved
- 1-2 heads of garlic, halved crosswise
- 1-2 celery stalks, cut into chunks
- 1-2 bell peppers, cut into chunks
- 3-4 bay leaves
- 1-2 cups Cajun or Creole seasoning (adjust to taste)
- Hot sauce (optional)
- Salt

Instructions:

Start by purging the crawfish: Rinse the live crawfish thoroughly in a large container or tub, then cover them with water and add salt (about 1 cup per gallon of water). Allow the crawfish to soak for about 20-30 minutes to purge any impurities.

Meanwhile, fill a large stockpot or outdoor boiling pot with water and bring it to a rolling boil over high heat.

Once the water is boiling, add the Cajun or Creole seasoning, halved lemons, quartered onions, halved garlic heads, celery, bell peppers, and bay leaves to the pot. Let the mixture simmer for about 10-15 minutes to infuse the water with flavor.

Add the potatoes to the pot and cook for about 10 minutes.

Next, add the smoked sausage and corn on the cob to the pot and cook for another 5 minutes.

Carefully add the live crawfish to the pot and stir to ensure they are fully submerged.

Bring the water back to a boil and cook the crawfish for about 5-7 minutes, or until they turn bright red and float to the surface.

Turn off the heat and let the crawfish soak in the seasoned water for an additional 15-20 minutes to absorb more flavor.

Once done, carefully remove the crawfish and other ingredients from the pot using a strainer or spider basket and transfer them to a large serving platter or table lined with newspaper or butcher paper.

Serve the crawfish boil hot, accompanied by additional Cajun seasoning and hot sauce for those who want to spice it up even more.

Enjoy your delicious and authentic crawfish boil feast with friends and family!

Crawfish boils are often served with sides like coleslaw, French bread, or hush puppies, and cold beverages like beer or iced tea. It's a fun and communal dining experience that captures the spirit of Southern hospitality.

Cajun Crab Dip

Ingredients:

- 8 ounces lump crab meat, drained and picked over for shells
- 8 ounces cream cheese, softened
- 1/2 cup mayonnaise
- 1/4 cup grated Parmesan cheese
- 1/4 cup grated cheddar cheese
- 2 green onions, finely chopped
- 1 tablespoon Worcestershire sauce
- 1 tablespoon lemon juice
- 1 teaspoon Cajun seasoning (adjust to taste)
- 1/2 teaspoon garlic powder
- 1/2 teaspoon onion powder
- 1/4 teaspoon paprika
- Salt and pepper to taste
- Chopped fresh parsley or green onions for garnish (optional)
- Crackers, bread, or vegetables for serving

Instructions:

Preheat the oven to 375°F (190°C).
In a mixing bowl, combine the softened cream cheese, mayonnaise, grated Parmesan cheese, grated cheddar cheese, chopped green onions, Worcestershire sauce, lemon juice, Cajun seasoning, garlic powder, onion powder, paprika, salt, and pepper. Mix well until smooth and creamy.
Gently fold in the lump crab meat until evenly distributed throughout the mixture.
Transfer the crab mixture to a baking dish or oven-safe skillet, spreading it out evenly.
Sprinkle additional grated cheese on top of the crab mixture, if desired.
Bake the Cajun crab dip in the preheated oven for 20-25 minutes, or until hot and bubbly and the top is lightly golden brown.
Once done, remove the crab dip from the oven and let it cool slightly.
Garnish the Cajun crab dip with chopped fresh parsley or green onions, if desired.
Serve the dip hot with crackers, bread, or vegetables for dipping.
Enjoy your delicious Cajun crab dip as a tasty appetizer or snack!

This Cajun crab dip can also be made ahead of time and reheated before serving. It's best enjoyed warm and creamy with plenty of flavor from the Cajun seasoning and lump crab meat. Adjust the amount of Cajun seasoning to suit your taste preferences for spice.

Cajun Cornbread

Ingredients:

- 1 cup yellow cornmeal
- 1 cup all-purpose flour
- 1 tablespoon baking powder
- 1 teaspoon salt
- 1/2 teaspoon baking soda
- 1 cup buttermilk
- 2 large eggs
- 1/4 cup melted butter or vegetable oil
- 1/4 cup chopped green onions
- 1/4 cup chopped jalapeños (optional)
- 1/4 cup grated cheddar cheese (optional)
- 1 tablespoon Cajun seasoning
- 1 tablespoon honey or sugar (optional, for sweetness)

Instructions:

Preheat the oven to 400°F (200°C). Grease a 9x9-inch baking pan or cast-iron skillet with butter or oil.
In a large mixing bowl, combine the cornmeal, flour, baking powder, salt, baking soda, and Cajun seasoning. Stir until well combined.
In a separate bowl, whisk together the buttermilk, eggs, melted butter or oil, and honey or sugar (if using) until smooth.
Pour the wet ingredients into the dry ingredients and mix until just combined. Be careful not to overmix, as this can result in tough cornbread.
Fold in the chopped green onions, chopped jalapeños (if using), and grated cheddar cheese (if using) until evenly distributed throughout the batter.
Pour the batter into the prepared baking pan or skillet, spreading it out evenly.
Bake in the preheated oven for 20-25 minutes, or until the cornbread is golden brown on top and a toothpick inserted into the center comes out clean.
Once done, remove the cornbread from the oven and let it cool in the pan for a few minutes before slicing and serving.
Serve the Cajun cornbread warm as a side dish to your favorite Cajun or Southern-inspired meals.
Enjoy your delicious and flavorful Cajun cornbread!

This Cajun cornbread is perfect for serving alongside dishes like gumbo, jambalaya, or red beans and rice. The Cajun seasoning adds a spicy kick, while the green onions, jalapeños, and cheese add extra flavor and texture. Feel free to adjust the level of spiciness by adding more or less Cajun seasoning and jalapeños according to your taste preferences.

Cajun Dirty Shrimp

Ingredients:

- 1 pound large shrimp, peeled and deveined
- 2 tablespoons Cajun seasoning
- 2 tablespoons olive oil
- 4 cloves garlic, minced
- 1 onion, diced
- 1 bell pepper, diced
- 2 stalks celery, diced
- 1 can (14.5 ounces) diced tomatoes
- 1 cup chicken or seafood broth
- 1 teaspoon Worcestershire sauce
- 1 teaspoon hot sauce (adjust to taste)
- 1 teaspoon dried thyme
- 1 teaspoon dried oregano
- Salt and pepper to taste
- Cooked rice or pasta, for serving
- Chopped fresh parsley, for garnish (optional)

Instructions:

In a bowl, toss the peeled and deveined shrimp with Cajun seasoning until evenly coated. Set aside.

Heat olive oil in a large skillet over medium heat. Add minced garlic and cook for about 1 minute until fragrant.

Add diced onion, bell pepper, and celery to the skillet. Cook, stirring occasionally, for about 5-6 minutes until the vegetables are softened.

Stir in diced tomatoes (with their juices), chicken or seafood broth, Worcestershire sauce, hot sauce, dried thyme, and dried oregano. Season with salt and pepper to taste.

Bring the mixture to a simmer and let it cook for about 10-15 minutes, stirring occasionally, to allow the flavors to meld and the sauce to thicken slightly.

Once the sauce has thickened, add the seasoned shrimp to the skillet. Stir to coat the shrimp in the sauce.

Cook the shrimp for about 4-5 minutes, or until they are pink and opaque, stirring occasionally.

Once the shrimp are cooked through, remove the skillet from the heat.
Serve the Cajun Dirty Shrimp hot over cooked rice or pasta.
Garnish with chopped fresh parsley, if desired.
Enjoy your delicious and flavorful Cajun Dirty Shrimp!

This dish is perfect for a quick and easy weeknight dinner, and it's sure to impress with its bold flavors and spicy kick. Feel free to adjust the level of Cajun seasoning and hot sauce according to your taste preferences.

Cajun Shrimp Scampi

Ingredients:

- 1 pound large shrimp, peeled and deveined
- 8 ounces linguine or spaghetti
- 4 tablespoons unsalted butter
- 4 cloves garlic, minced
- 1 tablespoon Cajun seasoning
- 1/4 teaspoon red pepper flakes (adjust to taste)
- 1/4 cup dry white wine (optional)
- 1/4 cup chicken broth
- Juice of 1 lemon
- Zest of 1 lemon
- Salt and pepper to taste
- Chopped fresh parsley for garnish
- Grated Parmesan cheese for serving (optional)

Instructions:

Cook the linguine or spaghetti according to the package instructions until al dente. Drain and set aside.

In a large skillet, melt the butter over medium heat. Add the minced garlic and cook for about 1 minute until fragrant.

Add the Cajun seasoning and red pepper flakes to the skillet, stirring to combine with the butter and garlic.

Add the shrimp to the skillet and cook for 2-3 minutes on each side until they turn pink and opaque.

If using white wine, pour it into the skillet and let it simmer for a minute, scraping any browned bits from the bottom of the skillet.

Stir in the chicken broth, lemon juice, and lemon zest. Let the sauce simmer for another 2-3 minutes to allow the flavors to meld and the sauce to thicken slightly. Season with salt and pepper to taste.

Add the cooked linguine or spaghetti to the skillet, tossing to coat it evenly in the Cajun shrimp scampi sauce.

Once everything is well combined and heated through, remove the skillet from the heat.

Serve the Cajun Shrimp Scampi hot, garnished with chopped fresh parsley and grated Parmesan cheese if desired.
Enjoy your delicious and flavorful Cajun Shrimp Scampi!

This dish is perfect for a quick and easy weeknight dinner, and it's sure to impress with its bold Cajun flavors. Feel free to adjust the amount of Cajun seasoning and red pepper flakes according to your taste preferences for spice.

Cajun Crawfish Pie

Ingredients:

For the Filling:

- 1 pound crawfish tails, peeled and deveined
- 1 tablespoon olive oil
- 1 onion, finely chopped
- 1 bell pepper, finely chopped
- 2 celery stalks, finely chopped
- 2 cloves garlic, minced
- 1/2 cup diced tomatoes
- 1/2 cup chicken or seafood broth
- 1 teaspoon Cajun seasoning
- 1/2 teaspoon paprika
- 1/4 teaspoon cayenne pepper (optional, adjust to taste)
- Salt and pepper to taste
- 2 tablespoons chopped fresh parsley
- 1 tablespoon chopped green onions
- 1 tablespoon cornstarch (optional, for thickening)

For the Pie Crust:

- 1 9-inch pie crust (store-bought or homemade)

Instructions:

Preheat the oven to 375°F (190°C).
In a large skillet, heat the olive oil over medium heat. Add the chopped onion, bell pepper, and celery. Cook, stirring occasionally, for about 5-6 minutes, or until the vegetables are softened.
Add the minced garlic to the skillet and cook for an additional minute until fragrant.
Stir in the diced tomatoes, chicken or seafood broth, Cajun seasoning, paprika, cayenne pepper (if using), salt, and pepper. Bring the mixture to a simmer.

If desired, mix the cornstarch with a tablespoon of water to create a slurry. Stir the slurry into the simmering mixture to help thicken the sauce.

Add the crawfish tails to the skillet and cook for about 3-4 minutes, or until they are heated through and cooked.

Remove the skillet from the heat and stir in the chopped parsley and green onions. Taste and adjust seasoning if necessary.

Roll out the pie crust and line a 9-inch pie dish with it. Trim any excess dough from the edges.

Pour the crawfish filling into the prepared pie crust, spreading it out evenly.

If desired, sprinkle grated cheese on top of the filling.

Place the pie dish on a baking sheet and bake in the preheated oven for 25-30 minutes, or until the crust is golden brown and the filling is bubbly.

Once done, remove the Cajun Crawfish Pie from the oven and let it cool for a few minutes before slicing and serving.

Serve hot, garnished with additional chopped parsley or green onions if desired. Enjoy your delicious Cajun Crawfish Pie!

Feel free to customize this recipe by adding other ingredients such as diced bell peppers, mushrooms, or spinach to the filling. You can also adjust the level of spiciness by adding more or less Cajun seasoning and cayenne pepper according to your taste preferences.

Cajun Roasted Potatoes

Ingredients:

- 2 pounds baby potatoes (red or Yukon gold), washed and quartered
- 2 tablespoons olive oil
- 2 teaspoons Cajun seasoning
- 1 teaspoon paprika
- 1/2 teaspoon garlic powder
- 1/2 teaspoon onion powder
- 1/4 teaspoon cayenne pepper (optional, for extra heat)
- Salt and pepper to taste
- Chopped fresh parsley for garnish (optional)

Instructions:

Preheat the oven to 425°F (220°C). Line a baking sheet with parchment paper or aluminum foil for easy cleanup.
In a large bowl, toss the quartered baby potatoes with olive oil until evenly coated.
In a small bowl, mix together the Cajun seasoning, paprika, garlic powder, onion powder, cayenne pepper (if using), salt, and pepper.
Sprinkle the seasoning mixture over the potatoes, tossing to coat them evenly with the spices.
Arrange the seasoned potatoes in a single layer on the prepared baking sheet.
Roast the potatoes in the preheated oven for 25-30 minutes, or until they are golden brown and crispy on the outside, and tender on the inside. Stir the potatoes halfway through the cooking time to ensure even browning.
Once the Cajun roasted potatoes are done, remove them from the oven and transfer them to a serving dish.
Garnish the potatoes with chopped fresh parsley, if desired, for a pop of color and freshness.
Serve the Cajun roasted potatoes hot as a flavorful side dish alongside your favorite main course.
Enjoy your delicious and spicy Cajun roasted potatoes!

Feel free to adjust the amount of Cajun seasoning and cayenne pepper according to your taste preferences for spice. You can also add other seasonings or herbs like thyme or rosemary for additional flavor variations.

Cajun Blackened Salmon

Ingredients:

- 4 salmon fillets, skin-on or skinless (about 6 ounces each)
- 2 tablespoons Cajun seasoning (store-bought or homemade)
- 2 tablespoons olive oil or melted butter
- 1 tablespoon paprika
- 1 teaspoon garlic powder
- 1 teaspoon onion powder
- 1 teaspoon dried thyme
- 1/2 teaspoon cayenne pepper (adjust to taste)
- Salt and pepper to taste
- Lemon wedges for serving
- Fresh chopped parsley for garnish (optional)

Instructions:

In a small bowl, mix together the Cajun seasoning, paprika, garlic powder, onion powder, dried thyme, cayenne pepper, salt, and pepper.
Pat the salmon fillets dry with paper towels. Drizzle olive oil or melted butter over both sides of the salmon fillets.
Rub the Cajun seasoning mixture evenly over both sides of the salmon fillets, ensuring they are well coated with the seasoning blend.
Heat a large skillet or cast-iron skillet over medium-high heat until hot.
Carefully place the seasoned salmon fillets in the hot skillet, skin-side down if using skin-on fillets.
Cook the salmon fillets for about 3-4 minutes on each side, depending on the thickness of the fillets, until the spice rub forms a dark crust and the salmon is cooked through. The internal temperature of the salmon should reach 145°F (63°C).
Once the salmon is cooked to your desired doneness, remove the fillets from the skillet and transfer them to a serving platter.
Squeeze fresh lemon juice over the blackened salmon fillets and garnish with chopped fresh parsley, if desired.
Serve the Cajun blackened salmon hot with additional lemon wedges on the side. Enjoy your flavorful and spicy Cajun blackened salmon!

This Cajun blackened salmon pairs well with rice, quinoa, or roasted vegetables for a complete meal. Adjust the amount of cayenne pepper in the Cajun seasoning blend according to your desired level of spiciness.

Cajun Stuffed Peppers

Ingredients:

- 4 large bell peppers (any color), halved and seeds removed
- 1 cup long-grain white rice
- 2 cups chicken or vegetable broth
- 1 tablespoon olive oil
- 1 onion, finely chopped
- 2 cloves garlic, minced
- 1 bell pepper, finely chopped
- 2 stalks celery, finely chopped
- 8 ounces Andouille sausage, diced
- 8 ounces shrimp, peeled, deveined, and chopped
- 1 tablespoon Cajun seasoning
- 1 teaspoon paprika
- 1/2 teaspoon dried thyme
- Salt and pepper to taste
- 1 cup shredded cheddar cheese
- Chopped fresh parsley for garnish (optional)

Instructions:

Preheat the oven to 375°F (190°C). Lightly grease a baking dish large enough to hold the halved bell peppers.

In a medium saucepan, bring the chicken or vegetable broth to a boil. Stir in the rice, reduce the heat to low, cover, and simmer for 15-20 minutes, or until the rice is cooked and the liquid is absorbed. Remove from heat and set aside.

While the rice is cooking, heat olive oil in a large skillet over medium heat. Add the chopped onion, minced garlic, chopped bell pepper, and chopped celery. Cook, stirring occasionally, for about 5-6 minutes until the vegetables are softened.

Add the diced Andouille sausage to the skillet and cook for an additional 3-4 minutes until browned.

Stir in the chopped shrimp and cook for 2-3 minutes until they turn pink and opaque.

Add the Cajun seasoning, paprika, dried thyme, salt, and pepper to the skillet, stirring to coat the mixture evenly with the spices.

Remove the skillet from the heat and stir in the cooked rice until well combined.
Arrange the bell pepper halves in the prepared baking dish. Spoon the Cajun rice and sausage mixture evenly into each bell pepper half.
Sprinkle shredded cheddar cheese over the stuffed peppers.
Cover the baking dish with aluminum foil and bake in the preheated oven for 25-30 minutes, or until the peppers are tender and the filling is heated through.
Once done, remove the foil and bake for an additional 5-10 minutes until the cheese is melted and bubbly.
Remove the Cajun stuffed peppers from the oven and let them cool for a few minutes before serving.
Garnish with chopped fresh parsley, if desired.
Serve the Cajun stuffed peppers hot as a delicious and flavorful main dish.

Enjoy your Cajun stuffed peppers packed with savory Cajun flavors! You can customize this recipe by adding other ingredients such as diced tomatoes, corn, or black beans to the filling according to your taste preferences.

Cajun Seafood Pasta

Ingredients:

- 8 ounces fettuccine or linguine pasta
- 1 pound shrimp, peeled and deveined
- 1 pound scallops
- 8 ounces crab meat (fresh or canned)
- 4 tablespoons unsalted butter
- 4 cloves garlic, minced
- 1 onion, finely chopped
- 1 bell pepper, diced
- 2 stalks celery, diced
- 1 cup chicken or seafood broth
- 1 cup heavy cream
- 2 tablespoons Cajun seasoning
- 1 teaspoon paprika
- 1/2 teaspoon dried thyme
- Salt and pepper to taste
- Chopped fresh parsley for garnish
- Grated Parmesan cheese for serving (optional)

Instructions:

Cook the pasta according to the package instructions until al dente. Drain and set aside.

In a large skillet or saucepan, melt the butter over medium heat. Add the minced garlic, chopped onion, diced bell pepper, and diced celery. Cook, stirring occasionally, for about 5-6 minutes until the vegetables are softened.

Add the Cajun seasoning, paprika, dried thyme, salt, and pepper to the skillet, stirring to coat the vegetables evenly with the spices.

Pour the chicken or seafood broth into the skillet and bring it to a simmer. Let it cook for about 2-3 minutes to allow the flavors to meld.

Stir in the heavy cream and bring the mixture back to a simmer.

Add the shrimp, scallops, and crab meat to the skillet, stirring to coat them in the sauce. Cook for about 5-6 minutes, or until the seafood is cooked through and opaque.

Once the seafood is cooked, add the cooked pasta to the skillet, tossing to coat it evenly in the creamy Cajun seafood sauce.
Taste and adjust the seasoning with salt and pepper if necessary.
Once everything is well combined and heated through, remove the skillet from the heat.
Serve the Cajun seafood pasta hot, garnished with chopped fresh parsley and grated Parmesan cheese if desired.
Enjoy your delicious and flavorful Cajun seafood pasta!

This dish is perfect for a special occasion or a weeknight dinner, and it's sure to impress with its bold Cajun flavors. Feel free to adjust the amount of Cajun seasoning according to your taste preferences for spice.

Cajun Gumbo Soup

Ingredients:

- 1/2 cup vegetable oil or bacon drippings
- 1/2 cup all-purpose flour
- 1 onion, diced
- 1 bell pepper, diced
- 2 celery stalks, diced
- 4 cloves garlic, minced
- 1 pound Andouille sausage, sliced
- 1 pound chicken thighs, boneless and skinless, diced
- 1 pound shrimp, peeled and deveined
- 6 cups chicken or seafood broth
- 1 can (14.5 ounces) diced tomatoes
- 1 cup okra, sliced (fresh or frozen)
- 1 cup frozen sliced okra (optional)
- 2 bay leaves
- 2 teaspoons Cajun seasoning (adjust to taste)
- 1 teaspoon dried thyme
- 1/2 teaspoon paprika
- Salt and pepper to taste
- Cooked rice for serving
- Chopped fresh parsley and green onions for garnish

Instructions:

In a large Dutch oven or heavy-bottomed pot, heat the vegetable oil or bacon drippings over medium heat.

Once the oil is hot, gradually whisk in the flour to make a roux. Cook the roux, stirring constantly, until it turns a deep golden brown color, about 20-25 minutes. Be careful not to burn the roux.

Add the diced onion, bell pepper, celery, and minced garlic to the pot. Cook, stirring occasionally, for about 5-6 minutes until the vegetables are softened.

Stir in the sliced Andouille sausage and diced chicken thighs. Cook for an additional 5-6 minutes, or until the sausage and chicken are browned.

Add the diced tomatoes (with their juices), chicken or seafood broth, sliced okra, bay leaves, Cajun seasoning, dried thyme, paprika, salt, and pepper to the pot. Stir to combine.

Bring the gumbo to a simmer, then reduce the heat to low and let it simmer gently for about 30-40 minutes, stirring occasionally, to allow the flavors to meld and the gumbo to thicken slightly.

About 10 minutes before serving, add the peeled and deveined shrimp to the pot. Cook for 5-7 minutes, or until the shrimp are pink and opaque.

Taste the gumbo and adjust the seasoning with additional salt, pepper, or Cajun seasoning if necessary.

Once done, remove the bay leaves from the gumbo.

To serve, ladle the Cajun gumbo soup over cooked rice in bowls.

Garnish each serving with chopped fresh parsley and green onions.

Enjoy your delicious and flavorful Cajun gumbo soup!

This hearty and comforting dish is perfect for serving on a chilly evening or for entertaining guests. Feel free to customize the gumbo by adding other ingredients such as crab meat, oysters, or different types of sausage according to your taste preferences.

Creole Shrimp and Sausage Jambalaya

Ingredients:

- 1 pound large shrimp, peeled and deveined
- 8 ounces Andouille sausage, sliced
- 1 onion, diced
- 1 bell pepper, diced
- 2 celery stalks, diced
- 3 cloves garlic, minced
- 1 can (14.5 ounces) diced tomatoes
- 1 cup long-grain white rice
- 2 cups chicken broth
- 2 tablespoons tomato paste
- 2 tablespoons olive oil
- 2 teaspoons Creole seasoning
- 1 teaspoon paprika
- 1/2 teaspoon dried thyme
- 1/2 teaspoon dried oregano
- 1/4 teaspoon cayenne pepper (optional, for extra heat)
- Salt and pepper to taste
- Chopped fresh parsley for garnish

Instructions:

Heat olive oil in a large skillet or Dutch oven over medium-high heat.
Add the sliced Andouille sausage to the skillet and cook until browned, about 5-6 minutes.
Add the diced onion, bell pepper, and celery to the skillet. Cook, stirring occasionally, for about 5-6 minutes until the vegetables are softened.
Stir in the minced garlic and cook for an additional minute until fragrant.
Add the diced tomatoes (with their juices) and tomato paste to the skillet. Stir to combine.
Stir in the Creole seasoning, paprika, dried thyme, dried oregano, cayenne pepper (if using), salt, and pepper.
Add the rice to the skillet and stir until it is well coated with the vegetable and spice mixture.
Pour the chicken broth into the skillet and bring the mixture to a simmer.

Reduce the heat to low, cover, and let the jambalaya simmer for about 20-25 minutes, or until the rice is cooked and most of the liquid is absorbed.

Once the rice is cooked, stir in the peeled and deveined shrimp.

Cover the skillet again and cook for an additional 5-7 minutes, or until the shrimp are pink and opaque.

Once the shrimp are cooked through, remove the skillet from the heat.

Taste the jambalaya and adjust the seasoning with additional salt and pepper if necessary.

Garnish the Creole shrimp and sausage jambalaya with chopped fresh parsley before serving.

Serve hot and enjoy your flavorful Creole shrimp and sausage jambalaya!

This dish is perfect for a comforting and satisfying meal, and it's sure to impress with its bold Creole flavors. Adjust the amount of cayenne pepper in the recipe according to your desired level of spiciness.

Blackened Redfish

Ingredients:

- 4 redfish fillets, skin-on or skinless (about 6-8 ounces each)
- 4 tablespoons unsalted butter, melted
- 2 tablespoons Cajun seasoning
- 1 teaspoon paprika
- 1 teaspoon garlic powder
- 1 teaspoon onion powder
- 1/2 teaspoon dried thyme
- 1/2 teaspoon dried oregano
- 1/4 teaspoon cayenne pepper (adjust to taste)
- Salt and pepper to taste
- Lemon wedges for serving
- Chopped fresh parsley for garnish (optional)

Instructions:

In a small bowl, mix together the Cajun seasoning, paprika, garlic powder, onion powder, dried thyme, dried oregano, cayenne pepper, salt, and pepper.
Pat the redfish fillets dry with paper towels.
Brush both sides of each redfish fillet with melted butter.
Sprinkle the Cajun seasoning mixture evenly over both sides of the redfish fillets, pressing gently to adhere the seasoning.
Heat a large cast-iron skillet over high heat until very hot.
Carefully place the seasoned redfish fillets in the hot skillet, skin-side down if using skin-on fillets.
Cook the redfish fillets for about 2-3 minutes on each side, or until they are blackened and crispy on the outside and cooked through on the inside. The internal temperature of the fish should reach 145°F (63°C).
Once the redfish fillets are cooked, remove them from the skillet and transfer them to a serving platter.
Squeeze fresh lemon juice over the blackened redfish fillets and garnish with chopped fresh parsley, if desired.
Serve the blackened redfish hot with additional lemon wedges on the side.
Enjoy your delicious and flavorful blackened redfish!

This dish is perfect for a quick and easy weeknight dinner, and it's sure to impress with its bold Cajun flavors. Feel free to adjust the amount of Cajun seasoning and cayenne pepper according to your taste preferences for spice.

Cajun Chicken and Sausage Pasta

Ingredients:

- 8 ounces penne or fettuccine pasta
- 2 boneless, skinless chicken breasts, cut into bite-sized pieces
- 8 ounces Andouille sausage, sliced
- 1 tablespoon Cajun seasoning
- 2 tablespoons olive oil
- 1 onion, diced
- 1 bell pepper, diced
- 2 cloves garlic, minced
- 1 cup chicken broth
- 1 cup heavy cream
- 1 can (14.5 ounces) diced tomatoes
- 1 teaspoon paprika
- 1/2 teaspoon dried thyme
- Salt and pepper to taste
- Chopped fresh parsley for garnish
- Grated Parmesan cheese for serving (optional)

Instructions:

Cook the pasta according to the package instructions until al dente. Drain and set aside.
In a large skillet, heat the olive oil over medium-high heat.
Season the chicken breast pieces with Cajun seasoning.
Add the seasoned chicken to the skillet and cook for 5-6 minutes, or until browned and cooked through. Remove the chicken from the skillet and set aside.
In the same skillet, add the sliced Andouille sausage and cook for 3-4 minutes, or until browned. Remove the sausage from the skillet and set aside.
Add diced onion and bell pepper to the skillet. Cook for 4-5 minutes, or until softened.
Add minced garlic to the skillet and cook for an additional minute until fragrant.
Pour chicken broth into the skillet and bring to a simmer, scraping up any browned bits from the bottom of the skillet.
Stir in heavy cream, diced tomatoes (with their juices), paprika, dried thyme, salt, and pepper. Let the sauce simmer for 5-6 minutes, or until slightly thickened.

Add the cooked chicken and Andouille sausage back to the skillet. Stir to combine and let everything heat through.

Add the cooked pasta to the skillet and toss to coat evenly in the sauce.

Taste and adjust seasoning with salt and pepper if necessary.

Once everything is heated through, remove the skillet from the heat.

Serve the Cajun chicken and sausage pasta hot, garnished with chopped fresh parsley and grated Parmesan cheese if desired.

Enjoy your delicious and flavorful Cajun chicken and sausage pasta!

This dish is perfect for a satisfying weeknight dinner, and it's sure to impress with its bold Cajun flavors. Feel free to adjust the amount of Cajun seasoning according to your taste preferences for spice.

Cajun Shrimp Tacos

Ingredients:

For the Cajun Shrimp:

- 1 pound large shrimp, peeled and deveined
- 2 tablespoons olive oil
- 2 tablespoons Cajun seasoning
- 1 teaspoon paprika
- 1/2 teaspoon garlic powder
- 1/2 teaspoon onion powder
- 1/4 teaspoon cayenne pepper (adjust to taste)
- Salt and pepper to taste

For the Creamy Sauce:

- 1/2 cup mayonnaise
- 2 tablespoons sour cream or Greek yogurt
- 1 tablespoon fresh lime juice
- 1 teaspoon Cajun seasoning
- Salt and pepper to taste

For the Tacos:

- 8 small flour or corn tortillas
- Shredded lettuce
- Diced tomatoes
- Sliced avocado
- Sliced jalapeños (optional)
- Chopped fresh cilantro
- Lime wedges for serving

Instructions:

In a medium bowl, combine the Cajun seasoning, paprika, garlic powder, onion powder, cayenne pepper, salt, and pepper.

Add the peeled and deveined shrimp to the bowl and toss to coat them evenly with the Cajun seasoning mixture.

Heat olive oil in a large skillet over medium-high heat.

Once the skillet is hot, add the seasoned shrimp in a single layer. Cook for 2-3 minutes on each side, or until the shrimp are pink and opaque. Remove from heat and set aside.

In a small bowl, whisk together the mayonnaise, sour cream or Greek yogurt, fresh lime juice, Cajun seasoning, salt, and pepper to make the creamy sauce. Adjust seasoning to taste.

Warm the tortillas according to package instructions.

To assemble the tacos, place a spoonful of shredded lettuce on each tortilla. Top with Cajun shrimp, diced tomatoes, sliced avocado, sliced jalapeños (if using), and chopped fresh cilantro.

Drizzle the creamy sauce over the toppings.

Serve the Cajun shrimp tacos with lime wedges on the side for squeezing.

Enjoy your delicious and flavorful Cajun shrimp tacos!

These tacos are perfect for a quick and easy weeknight meal or for entertaining guests.

Feel free to customize the toppings and adjust the level of spiciness by adding more or less cayenne pepper according to your taste preferences.

Cajun Stuffed Chicken Breast

Ingredients:

For the Cajun Stuffing:

- 4 boneless, skinless chicken breasts
- 1 cup cooked rice
- 1/2 cup Andouille sausage, diced
- 1/2 cup bell pepper, diced
- 1/2 cup onion, diced
- 2 cloves garlic, minced
- 1 tablespoon Cajun seasoning
- Salt and pepper to taste
- 1 tablespoon olive oil
- 1/4 cup chicken broth (optional, for moisture)

For the Cajun Rub:

- 2 tablespoons Cajun seasoning
- 1 teaspoon paprika
- 1/2 teaspoon garlic powder
- 1/2 teaspoon onion powder
- 1/4 teaspoon cayenne pepper (optional, adjust to taste)
- Salt and pepper to taste

Instructions:

Preheat your oven to 375°F (190°C).
In a skillet, heat olive oil over medium heat. Add diced Andouille sausage and cook until lightly browned, about 3-4 minutes.
Add diced bell pepper and onion to the skillet and cook until softened, about 4-5 minutes. Add minced garlic and cook for an additional minute until fragrant. Remove from heat and set aside.
In a mixing bowl, combine the cooked rice with the sausage and vegetable mixture. Season with Cajun seasoning, salt, and pepper. If the stuffing seems dry, you can add a little chicken broth to moisten it.
Prepare the Cajun rub by mixing Cajun seasoning, paprika, garlic powder, onion powder, cayenne pepper, salt, and pepper in a small bowl.

Cut a slit horizontally along the side of each chicken breast to create a pocket for the stuffing. Be careful not to cut all the way through.

Season the inside of each chicken breast with the Cajun rub, making sure to coat both sides.

Stuff each chicken breast with the Cajun rice and sausage mixture, pressing down gently to seal.

Season the outside of each chicken breast with the remaining Cajun rub.

Place the stuffed chicken breasts in a baking dish lined with parchment paper or lightly greased.

Bake in the preheated oven for 25-30 minutes, or until the chicken is cooked through and the internal temperature reaches 165°F (74°C).

Once done, remove the Cajun stuffed chicken breasts from the oven and let them rest for a few minutes before serving.

Serve the Cajun stuffed chicken breasts hot, garnished with chopped fresh parsley or green onions if desired.

Enjoy your delicious and flavorful Cajun stuffed chicken breast!

This dish pairs well with a side of vegetables or a fresh salad for a complete meal. Feel free to customize the stuffing with your favorite ingredients or adjust the level of spiciness according to your taste preferences.

Cajun Baked Catfish

Ingredients:

- 4 catfish fillets (about 6-8 ounces each)
- 2 tablespoons olive oil
- 2 tablespoons Cajun seasoning
- 1 teaspoon paprika
- 1 teaspoon garlic powder
- 1 teaspoon onion powder
- 1/2 teaspoon dried thyme
- 1/2 teaspoon dried oregano
- 1/4 teaspoon cayenne pepper (adjust to taste)
- Salt and pepper to taste
- Lemon wedges for serving
- Chopped fresh parsley for garnish (optional)

Instructions:

Preheat your oven to 375°F (190°C). Lightly grease a baking dish large enough to hold the catfish fillets in a single layer.
In a small bowl, combine the Cajun seasoning, paprika, garlic powder, onion powder, dried thyme, dried oregano, cayenne pepper, salt, and pepper.
Pat the catfish fillets dry with paper towels.
Brush both sides of each catfish fillet with olive oil.
Sprinkle the Cajun seasoning mixture evenly over both sides of the catfish fillets, pressing gently to adhere the seasoning.
Place the seasoned catfish fillets in the prepared baking dish.
Bake in the preheated oven for 20-25 minutes, or until the catfish is cooked through and flakes easily with a fork. The internal temperature of the fish should reach 145°F (63°C).
Once done, remove the Cajun baked catfish from the oven and let it rest for a few minutes.
Serve the Cajun baked catfish hot, garnished with chopped fresh parsley and lemon wedges for squeezing.
Enjoy your delicious and flavorful Cajun baked catfish!

This dish pairs well with sides such as rice, steamed vegetables, or a fresh salad. Feel free to adjust the amount of Cajun seasoning and cayenne pepper according to your taste preferences for spice.

Cajun Grilled Shrimp Skewers

Ingredients:

- 1 pound large shrimp, peeled and deveined
- 2 tablespoons olive oil
- 2 tablespoons Cajun seasoning
- 1 teaspoon paprika
- 1/2 teaspoon garlic powder
- 1/2 teaspoon onion powder
- 1/4 teaspoon dried thyme
- 1/4 teaspoon dried oregano
- 1/4 teaspoon cayenne pepper (adjust to taste)
- Salt and pepper to taste
- Wooden or metal skewers, soaked in water for 30 minutes if using wooden ones
- Lemon wedges for serving
- Chopped fresh parsley for garnish (optional)

Instructions:

Preheat your grill to medium-high heat.
In a small bowl, combine the Cajun seasoning, paprika, garlic powder, onion powder, dried thyme, dried oregano, cayenne pepper, salt, and pepper.
Pat the peeled and deveined shrimp dry with paper towels.
Thread the shrimp onto skewers, ensuring they are evenly spaced and not overcrowded.
Brush both sides of the shrimp skewers with olive oil.
Sprinkle the Cajun seasoning mixture evenly over both sides of the shrimp skewers, pressing gently to adhere the seasoning.
Place the shrimp skewers on the preheated grill and cook for 2-3 minutes on each side, or until the shrimp are pink and opaque with grill marks.
Once done, remove the Cajun grilled shrimp skewers from the grill and transfer them to a serving platter.
Squeeze fresh lemon juice over the grilled shrimp skewers and garnish with chopped fresh parsley, if desired.
Serve the Cajun grilled shrimp skewers hot as a delicious appetizer or main dish.
Enjoy your flavorful and perfectly grilled Cajun shrimp skewers!

These Cajun grilled shrimp skewers are perfect for summer cookouts, parties, or as a quick and easy weeknight meal. Feel free to adjust the amount of Cajun seasoning and cayenne pepper according to your taste preferences for spice.

Cajun Chicken and Rice

Ingredients:

- 1 pound boneless, skinless chicken breasts, cut into bite-sized pieces
- 2 tablespoons Cajun seasoning
- 2 tablespoons olive oil
- 1 onion, diced
- 1 bell pepper, diced
- 2 cloves garlic, minced
- 1 cup long-grain white rice
- 2 cups chicken broth
- 1 can (14.5 ounces) diced tomatoes
- 1 teaspoon paprika
- 1/2 teaspoon dried thyme
- Salt and pepper to taste
- Chopped fresh parsley for garnish

Instructions:

In a mixing bowl, toss the bite-sized chicken pieces with Cajun seasoning until evenly coated.
Heat olive oil in a large skillet or Dutch oven over medium-high heat.
Add the seasoned chicken pieces to the skillet and cook for 5-6 minutes, or until browned and cooked through. Remove the chicken from the skillet and set aside.
In the same skillet, add diced onion and bell pepper. Cook for 4-5 minutes, or until softened.
Add minced garlic to the skillet and cook for an additional minute until fragrant.
Stir in the uncooked rice, diced tomatoes (with their juices), chicken broth, paprika, dried thyme, salt, and pepper.
Bring the mixture to a simmer, then reduce the heat to low.
Cover the skillet and let the rice simmer for 18-20 minutes, or until the rice is cooked and most of the liquid is absorbed.
Once the rice is cooked, return the cooked chicken to the skillet and stir to combine with the rice mixture.
Let the chicken and rice mixture heat through for a few minutes.
Taste and adjust the seasoning with additional salt and pepper if necessary.
Once done, remove the skillet from the heat.
Serve the Cajun chicken and rice hot, garnished with chopped fresh parsley.

Enjoy your delicious and flavorful Cajun chicken and rice!

This dish is perfect for a satisfying weeknight dinner, and it's sure to impress with its bold Cajun flavors. Feel free to customize the dish by adding other vegetables such as celery or corn, or by adjusting the level of spiciness according to your taste preferences.

Cajun Shrimp and Sausage Gumbo

Ingredients:

For the Roux:

- 1/2 cup vegetable oil or bacon drippings
- 1/2 cup all-purpose flour

For the Gumbo:

- 1 pound large shrimp, peeled and deveined
- 1/2 pound Andouille sausage, sliced
- 1 onion, diced
- 1 bell pepper, diced
- 2 stalks celery, diced
- 4 cloves garlic, minced
- 1 can (14.5 ounces) diced tomatoes
- 6 cups chicken or seafood broth
- 1 teaspoon Cajun seasoning
- 1 teaspoon paprika
- 1/2 teaspoon dried thyme
- 1/2 teaspoon dried oregano
- 1/4 teaspoon cayenne pepper (adjust to taste)
- Salt and pepper to taste
- Cooked white rice for serving
- Chopped fresh parsley for garnish
- File powder (optional, for serving)

Instructions:

In a large Dutch oven or heavy-bottomed pot, heat the vegetable oil or bacon drippings over medium heat.
Gradually whisk in the flour to make a roux. Cook the roux, stirring constantly, until it turns a dark caramel color, about 20-25 minutes. Be careful not to burn the roux.

Once the roux is ready, add the diced onion, bell pepper, and celery to the pot. Cook, stirring occasionally, for about 5-6 minutes until the vegetables are softened.

Add minced garlic to the pot and cook for an additional minute until fragrant.

Stir in the sliced Andouille sausage and cook for 3-4 minutes until browned.

Add the diced tomatoes (with their juices) to the pot, stirring to combine.

Pour the chicken or seafood broth into the pot and bring the mixture to a simmer.

Stir in the Cajun seasoning, paprika, dried thyme, dried oregano, cayenne pepper, salt, and pepper.

Let the gumbo simmer for about 30-40 minutes, stirring occasionally, to allow the flavors to meld and the gumbo to thicken.

Once the gumbo has thickened to your desired consistency, add the peeled and deveined shrimp to the pot. Cook for 5-7 minutes, or until the shrimp are pink and opaque.

Taste the gumbo and adjust the seasoning with additional salt, pepper, or Cajun seasoning if necessary.

Once done, remove the pot from the heat.

To serve, ladle the Cajun shrimp and sausage gumbo over cooked white rice in bowls.

Garnish each serving with chopped fresh parsley and a sprinkle of file powder, if desired.

Enjoy your delicious and flavorful Cajun shrimp and sausage gumbo!

This dish is perfect for a comforting and satisfying meal, especially served with crusty French bread for dipping. Adjust the level of spiciness by adding more or less cayenne pepper according to your taste preferences.

Cajun Crab Salad

Ingredients:

For the Dressing:

- 1/4 cup mayonnaise
- 2 tablespoons Creole or Dijon mustard
- 1 tablespoon lemon juice
- 1 teaspoon Cajun seasoning
- 1/2 teaspoon paprika
- 1/4 teaspoon garlic powder
- Salt and pepper to taste

For the Salad:

- 1 pound lump crab meat, picked over for shells
- 1/2 cup diced bell pepper (red, green, or yellow)
- 1/4 cup diced celery
- 1/4 cup diced red onion
- 2 tablespoons chopped fresh parsley
- 1 tablespoon chopped green onions (optional)
- Salt and pepper to taste
- Lettuce leaves, for serving (optional)
- Lemon wedges, for serving

Instructions:

In a small bowl, whisk together the mayonnaise, mustard, lemon juice, Cajun seasoning, paprika, garlic powder, salt, and pepper to make the dressing. Adjust seasoning to taste.

In a large mixing bowl, combine the lump crab meat, diced bell pepper, diced celery, diced red onion, chopped fresh parsley, and chopped green onions (if using).

Pour the dressing over the crab and vegetable mixture. Gently toss until everything is evenly coated in the dressing.

Taste the salad and adjust the seasoning with additional salt, pepper, or Cajun seasoning if necessary.

Cover the bowl with plastic wrap and refrigerate the Cajun crab salad for at least 30 minutes to allow the flavors to meld.

Once chilled, serve the Cajun crab salad on a bed of lettuce leaves, if desired, and garnish with lemon wedges.

Enjoy your delicious and flavorful Cajun crab salad as a refreshing appetizer or light meal!

This salad is perfect for a summer gathering, picnic, or as a light lunch. Feel free to customize the salad by adding other ingredients such as diced avocado, cucumber, or cherry tomatoes according to your taste preferences.

Cajun Shrimp and Sausage Skillet

Ingredients:

- 1 pound large shrimp, peeled and deveined
- 1/2 pound Andouille sausage, sliced
- 2 tablespoons olive oil
- 1 onion, diced
- 1 bell pepper, diced
- 2 cloves garlic, minced
- 1 can (14.5 ounces) diced tomatoes
- 1 teaspoon Cajun seasoning
- 1/2 teaspoon paprika
- 1/2 teaspoon dried thyme
- 1/4 teaspoon dried oregano
- Salt and pepper to taste
- Cooked white rice for serving
- Chopped fresh parsley for garnish
- Lemon wedges for serving

Instructions:

Heat olive oil in a large skillet over medium-high heat.
Add the sliced Andouille sausage to the skillet and cook for 3-4 minutes, or until browned.
Add diced onion and bell pepper to the skillet. Cook for 4-5 minutes, or until softened.
Add minced garlic to the skillet and cook for an additional minute until fragrant.
Stir in the diced tomatoes (with their juices), Cajun seasoning, paprika, dried thyme, dried oregano, salt, and pepper. Let the mixture simmer for 5-6 minutes.
Add the peeled and deveined shrimp to the skillet. Cook for 3-4 minutes, or until the shrimp are pink and opaque.
Once done, remove the skillet from the heat.
Serve the Cajun shrimp and sausage skillet over cooked white rice.
Garnish with chopped fresh parsley and serve with lemon wedges on the side.
Enjoy your delicious and flavorful Cajun shrimp and sausage skillet!

This dish is perfect for a quick and easy weeknight meal, and it's sure to impress with its bold Cajun flavors. Feel free to adjust the level of spiciness by adding more or less Cajun seasoning according to your taste preferences.

Creole Stuffed Bell Peppers

Ingredients:

- 4 large bell peppers (any color), halved and seeds removed
- 1 tablespoon olive oil
- 1 onion, diced
- 2 cloves garlic, minced
- 1 pound ground beef or turkey
- 1 cup cooked rice
- 1 can (14.5 ounces) diced tomatoes, drained
- 1/2 cup tomato sauce
- 1 teaspoon Creole seasoning
- 1/2 teaspoon paprika
- 1/2 teaspoon dried thyme
- Salt and pepper to taste
- 1/2 cup shredded cheese (cheddar, Monterey Jack, or your choice)
- Chopped fresh parsley for garnish

Instructions:

Preheat your oven to 375°F (190°C). Lightly grease a baking dish large enough to hold the bell pepper halves.
In a large skillet, heat olive oil over medium heat.
Add diced onion to the skillet and cook for 4-5 minutes, or until softened.
Add minced garlic to the skillet and cook for an additional minute until fragrant.
Add ground beef or turkey to the skillet. Cook, breaking up the meat with a spoon, until browned and cooked through.
Stir in cooked rice, diced tomatoes, tomato sauce, Creole seasoning, paprika, dried thyme, salt, and pepper. Cook for 3-4 minutes to allow the flavors to meld.
Taste the filling and adjust seasoning if necessary.
Arrange the bell pepper halves in the prepared baking dish, cut side up.
Spoon the filling mixture evenly into each bell pepper half, pressing down gently to fill.
Sprinkle shredded cheese over the top of each stuffed bell pepper half.
Cover the baking dish with aluminum foil and bake in the preheated oven for 25-30 minutes, or until the peppers are tender and the filling is heated through.

Once done, remove the foil from the baking dish and switch the oven to broil. Broil the stuffed bell peppers for 2-3 minutes, or until the cheese is bubbly and lightly browned.

Remove the baking dish from the oven and let the stuffed bell peppers cool for a few minutes.

Garnish the Creole stuffed bell peppers with chopped fresh parsley before serving.

Enjoy your delicious and flavorful Creole stuffed bell peppers as a satisfying main dish!

These stuffed bell peppers are perfect for a family dinner or entertaining guests. Feel free to customize the filling with your favorite ingredients or adjust the level of spiciness according to your taste preferences.

Cajun Sausage and Shrimp Alfredo

Ingredients:

- 8 ounces fettuccine or your choice of pasta
- 1 tablespoon olive oil
- 1/2 pound Cajun-style Andouille sausage, sliced
- 1 pound large shrimp, peeled and deveined
- 3 cloves garlic, minced
- 1 teaspoon Cajun seasoning
- 1/2 teaspoon paprika
- 1/2 teaspoon dried thyme
- 1/2 cup chicken broth
- 1 cup heavy cream
- 1/2 cup grated Parmesan cheese
- Salt and pepper to taste
- Chopped fresh parsley for garnish
- Lemon wedges for serving (optional)

Instructions:

Cook the fettuccine according to the package instructions until al dente. Drain and set aside.
In a large skillet, heat olive oil over medium-high heat.
Add the sliced Cajun-style Andouille sausage to the skillet. Cook for 3-4 minutes, or until browned.
Add the peeled and deveined shrimp to the skillet. Cook for 2-3 minutes on each side, or until pink and opaque. Remove the shrimp from the skillet and set aside.
In the same skillet, add minced garlic and cook for about 1 minute until fragrant.
Stir in Cajun seasoning, paprika, and dried thyme. Cook for another minute to toast the spices.
Pour chicken broth into the skillet, scraping up any browned bits from the bottom of the pan.
Reduce the heat to medium-low and stir in heavy cream. Let the sauce simmer for about 5 minutes, or until slightly thickened.
Stir in grated Parmesan cheese until melted and incorporated into the sauce.
Taste the sauce and adjust the seasoning with salt and pepper if necessary.

Add the cooked fettuccine, Cajun sausage, and shrimp back to the skillet. Toss everything together until well coated in the sauce.

Once everything is heated through, remove the skillet from the heat.

Serve the Cajun sausage and shrimp Alfredo hot, garnished with chopped fresh parsley and lemon wedges if desired.

Enjoy your delicious and flavorful Cajun sausage and shrimp Alfredo!

This dish is perfect for a special occasion or a cozy dinner at home. Feel free to adjust the level of spiciness by adding more or less Cajun seasoning according to your taste preferences.

Cajun Shrimp and Sausage Pasta Bake

Ingredients:

- 8 ounces penne or your choice of pasta
- 1 tablespoon olive oil
- 1/2 pound Cajun-style Andouille sausage, sliced
- 1 pound large shrimp, peeled and deveined
- 1 onion, diced
- 1 bell pepper, diced
- 2 cloves garlic, minced
- 1 can (14.5 ounces) diced tomatoes, drained
- 1 cup chicken broth
- 1 cup heavy cream
- 1 tablespoon Cajun seasoning
- 1/2 teaspoon paprika
- Salt and pepper to taste
- 1 cup shredded cheese (cheddar, Monterey Jack, or your choice)
- Chopped fresh parsley for garnish

Instructions:

Preheat your oven to 375°F (190°C). Lightly grease a 9x13-inch baking dish.
Cook the pasta according to the package instructions until al dente. Drain and set aside.
In a large skillet, heat olive oil over medium-high heat.
Add the sliced Cajun-style Andouille sausage to the skillet. Cook for 3-4 minutes, or until browned.
Add the peeled and deveined shrimp to the skillet. Cook for 2-3 minutes on each side, or until pink and opaque. Remove the shrimp and sausage from the skillet and set aside.
In the same skillet, add diced onion and bell pepper. Cook for 4-5 minutes, or until softened.
Add minced garlic to the skillet and cook for an additional minute until fragrant.
Stir in diced tomatoes (with their juices), chicken broth, heavy cream, Cajun seasoning, paprika, salt, and pepper. Bring the mixture to a simmer and cook for 5-6 minutes, or until slightly thickened.

Add the cooked pasta, cooked shrimp, and sausage to the skillet. Stir until everything is well coated in the sauce.

Transfer the mixture to the prepared baking dish and spread it out evenly.

Sprinkle shredded cheese over the top of the pasta mixture.

Cover the baking dish with aluminum foil and bake in the preheated oven for 20-25 minutes.

Once done, remove the foil from the baking dish and switch the oven to broil. Broil the pasta bake for 2-3 minutes, or until the cheese is bubbly and lightly browned.

Remove the baking dish from the oven and let the pasta bake cool for a few minutes.

Garnish with chopped fresh parsley before serving.

Enjoy your delicious and flavorful Cajun shrimp and sausage pasta bake!

This dish is perfect for a comforting and satisfying meal, especially served with garlic bread and a side salad. Feel free to adjust the level of spiciness by adding more or less Cajun seasoning according to your taste preferences.

Cajun Fried Oysters

Ingredients:

- 1 dozen fresh oysters, shucked
- 1 cup all-purpose flour
- 1 teaspoon Cajun seasoning (adjust to taste)
- 1/2 teaspoon paprika
- 1/2 teaspoon garlic powder
- 1/2 teaspoon onion powder
- 1/4 teaspoon cayenne pepper (adjust to taste)
- Salt and pepper to taste
- 2 eggs
- 2 tablespoons milk or buttermilk
- Vegetable oil for frying
- Lemon wedges for serving
- Cocktail sauce or remoulade sauce for dipping (optional)

Instructions:

Rinse the shucked oysters under cold water and pat them dry with paper towels. Set aside.
In a shallow dish or bowl, combine the all-purpose flour, Cajun seasoning, paprika, garlic powder, onion powder, cayenne pepper, salt, and pepper. Mix well to combine.
In another shallow dish or bowl, whisk together the eggs and milk or buttermilk.
Heat vegetable oil in a deep fryer or large skillet to 350°F (175°C).
Dredge each oyster in the seasoned flour mixture, shaking off any excess.
Dip the floured oysters into the egg mixture, allowing any excess to drip off.
Dredge the oysters once again in the seasoned flour mixture, ensuring they are evenly coated.
Carefully place the coated oysters into the hot oil, a few at a time, making sure not to overcrowd the pan.
Fry the oysters for 2-3 minutes, or until they are golden brown and crispy, turning them halfway through the cooking time.
Once the oysters are cooked to a golden brown color, use a slotted spoon or tongs to transfer them to a plate lined with paper towels to drain excess oil.
Repeat the frying process with the remaining oysters.

Once all the oysters are fried, serve them hot with lemon wedges for squeezing and cocktail sauce or remoulade sauce for dipping, if desired.
Enjoy your delicious and crispy Cajun fried oysters as a tasty appetizer or main dish!

These Cajun fried oysters are best served hot and crispy, so enjoy them immediately after frying. They make a fantastic addition to seafood platters or as a flavorful appetizer for parties and gatherings. Adjust the level of spiciness by adding more or less Cajun seasoning and cayenne pepper according to your taste preferences.

Cajun Blackened Chicken

Ingredients:

- 4 boneless, skinless chicken breasts
- 2 tablespoons olive oil or melted butter
- Cajun seasoning (see below for homemade blend)
- Salt to taste

Cajun Seasoning:

- 2 tablespoons paprika
- 1 tablespoon garlic powder
- 1 tablespoon onion powder
- 1 tablespoon dried thyme
- 1 tablespoon dried oregano
- 1 teaspoon cayenne pepper (adjust to taste)
- 1 teaspoon black pepper
- 1 teaspoon white pepper
- 1 teaspoon smoked paprika (optional, for extra flavor)

Instructions:

In a small bowl, combine all the ingredients for the Cajun seasoning. Mix well to combine.

Pat the chicken breasts dry with paper towels. Season both sides of the chicken breasts with salt.

Generously coat both sides of each chicken breast with the Cajun seasoning mixture. Press the seasoning into the chicken to adhere.

Heat a large skillet over medium-high heat. Add olive oil or melted butter to the skillet.

Once the skillet is hot, carefully add the seasoned chicken breasts to the skillet. Cook for 5-6 minutes on each side, or until the chicken is cooked through and blackened on the outside. The internal temperature of the chicken should reach 165°F (74°C).

Remove the blackened chicken breasts from the skillet and let them rest for a few minutes before serving.

Serve the Cajun blackened chicken hot, garnished with fresh parsley or green onions if desired.

Enjoy your flavorful and spicy Cajun blackened chicken!

You can serve Cajun blackened chicken with a side of vegetables, rice, or salad for a complete meal. Adjust the level of spiciness by adding more or less cayenne pepper according to your taste preferences. This dish is perfect for a quick and easy weeknight dinner or for entertaining guests with its bold flavors.

Creole-style BBQ Shrimp

Ingredients:

- 1 pound large shrimp, peeled and deveined
- 1/2 cup unsalted butter, melted
- 1/4 cup Worcestershire sauce
- 2 tablespoons hot sauce (such as Tabasco)
- 2 tablespoons lemon juice
- 4 cloves garlic, minced
- 1 tablespoon Creole seasoning
- 1 teaspoon paprika
- 1 teaspoon dried thyme
- 1 teaspoon dried oregano
- 1/2 teaspoon black pepper
- 1/2 teaspoon cayenne pepper (adjust to taste)
- Salt to taste
- Lemon wedges, for serving
- Crusty bread, for serving

Instructions:

Preheat your oven to 400°F (200°C).
In a large mixing bowl, whisk together the melted butter, Worcestershire sauce, hot sauce, lemon juice, minced garlic, Creole seasoning, paprika, dried thyme, dried oregano, black pepper, cayenne pepper, and salt.
Add the peeled and deveined shrimp to the bowl with the sauce. Toss until the shrimp are evenly coated in the sauce.
Transfer the shrimp and sauce mixture to a baking dish or cast-iron skillet.
Bake in the preheated oven for 10-12 minutes, or until the shrimp are pink and cooked through, and the sauce is bubbling.
Once done, remove the baking dish or skillet from the oven.
Serve the Creole-style BBQ shrimp hot, garnished with chopped fresh parsley and lemon wedges.
Enjoy your flavorful and tangy Creole-style BBQ shrimp with crusty bread for dipping!

This dish is perfect for a special occasion or gathering with its bold flavors and easy preparation. The tangy and spicy sauce pairs perfectly with the tender and succulent shrimp. Adjust the level of spiciness by adding more or less cayenne pepper and hot sauce according to your taste preferences.